# GUIDE TO
# STAMP
## COLLECTING

# GUIDE TO
# STAMP
## COLLECTING

BY JANET KLUG

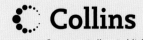

## Collins

An Imprint of HarperCollinsPublishers

*For the ever-patient Russ,*
*the guy who collected the collector*

*and*

*in memory of*
*W. Wilson Hulme II, Curator of Philately*
*Smithsonian National Postal Museum*
*2002–2006*

GUIDE TO STAMP COLLECTING. Copyright © 2008 by HarperCollins Publishers. All rights reserved. Printed in China. No part of this book may be used or reproduced in any manner whatsoever without written permission except in the case of brief quotations embodied in critical articles and reviews. For information, address HarperCollins Publishers, 10 East 53rd Street, New York, NY 10022.

HarperCollins books may be purchased for educational, business, or sales promotional use. For information please write: Special Markets Department, HarperCollins Publishers, 10 East 53rd Street, New York, NY 10022.

FIRST EDITION

The name of the "Smithsonian," "Smithsonian Institution," and the sunburst logo are registered trademarks of the Smithsonian Institution.

Produced by BAND-F Ltd, www.band-f.com
President / Partner: f-stop fitzgerald
Director of Development: Karen Jones
Production Editor: Mie Kingsley
Production Manager and Interior Design: Maria Fernandez
Digital Art Technician: Weston Minissali

Images on pages vii, 54, 58, 61, 63, 66, 67, 70, 71, 81, and 136 copyright f-stop Fitzgerald, Inc.
Stamp images on pages ii, 34, 57, 68, 72, 73, 75, and 104 are from the author's collection, photographed by f-stop Fitzgerald.
All images herein that are not specifically credited are courtesy of the author, Janet Klug.

Library of Congress Cataloging-in-Publication Data

Klug, Janet.
  Guide to stamp collecting / by Janet Klug. -- 1st ed.
      p. cm.
  Includes bibliographical references.
  ISBN 978-0-06-134139-7
  1. Stamp collecting--Handbooks, manuals, etc.  I. Title.

  HE6215.K58 2007
  769.56--dc22

2007027770

08 09 10 11 12    TOP    10  9  8  7  6  5  4  3  2  1

# CONTENTS

# PREFACE

Come explore the world of philately! If you are reading this page, you are already on your way to becoming a stamp collector.

The hobby of stamp collecting has something for people of all ages. Whether you are a student learning geography, a parent or teacher providing new ways to understand history and culture, a business professional seeking a stress reducer, or a retiree ready for a unique, creative challenge, stamp collecting offers you a hobby that is distinct, challenging, and infinitely rewarding. Traveling, bird watching, genealogy, art . . . stamp collecting speaks to countless interests and provides a corresponding opportunity for lifelong learning. Whatever your interests, budget, or location, you can design your collection to reflect your personality.

This book is the result of collaboration between author Janet Klug, a dedicated and enthusiastic stamp collector par excellence, and the Smithsonian National Postal Museum, home of America's National Stamp Collection. The result should not only help you begin your stamp collection but also serve as a reference and guide for many years of hobby enjoyment.

ALLEN R. KANE
DIRECTOR
SMITHSONIAN NATIONAL POSTAL MUSEUM

COLOR PLATE III C - 11. 1: Examples of color changes which can be induce
chemical or physical stresses.

# INTRODUCTION

Who hasn't paid a visit to a post office to buy stamps? We use stamps to send payments for bills and letters to clients. Brides seek out beautiful stamps to use on wedding invitations. New parents want special stamps for birth announcements. Nearly everyone likes to use attractive stamps for mailing greeting cards. Advertisers understand that mail bearing colorful stamps is far more likely to be opened and read. Stamps are everywhere—and yet they are often taken for granted.

## What Are Stamps?

Postage stamps are receipts that show payment has been made to a postal administration for delivery of a letter or for other postal services. To stamp collectors, stamps are much more than that. Postage stamps are visual representations of history. Stamps portray the geographic and cultural diversity of nations. They promote trade and tourism, honor national heroes, draw attention to social issues, and even raise money for worthy causes.

These are big and important jobs to entrust to tiny pieces of paper. Postal administrations the world over take them seriously, and entrust the design and printing of stamps to the finest artists and craftsmen. They create postage stamps that will serve as goodwill ambassadors as they travel from one country to another. It is this aspect of stamps that captures the attention of those who collect them.

Sweden and the United States issued stamps with complementary designs in stamp booklets for two international stamp collector shows held in 1986. The Swedish stamps are shown here.

## Why Collect Them?

Collecting stamps is not just a paper chase, although there is a thrill to be had in the hunt for elusive examples. Stamp collectors are intrigued by the people, places, and objects illustrated on stamps. They want to know more about the country that issued the stamp, who designed it, how it was printed, and how it was used. All of these elements combine to make stamp collecting a hobby that engages the mind, brings history to life, exercises creativity, and satisfies the desire to acquire beautiful objects. Best of all, stamp collecting is fun.

Stamp collecting has another advantage that is missing in many other hobbies. It can be enjoyed on any budget, including a nearly nonexistent one. The general public hears about a very small number of stamps that sell at auction for hundreds of thousands of dollars. But these are rare gems in the world of stamp collecting; they are the exceptions and not the rule.

## What Stamp Collecting Offers

Your mental image of a stamp collector might be that of a person hunched over a heavy album inserting stamps or peering through a thick magnifying glass to examine the album's contents. Your images are correct ones, but they are not the only ones.

Those who have been collecting stamps for a while will tell you that stamps are a relaxing and enjoyable way to learn about world history and cultures. Some stamp collectors collect because of their interest in the topic depicted on the stamp, such as trains, teddy bears, or tennis. Most collectors will tell you that stamps are miniature works of exquisite art and will appreciate them for their sheer beauty, and everyone who collects stamps will tell you it is fun.

Stamp collecting can be an escape from the daily hustle and bustle. It can be enjoyed in solitude, but also provides ample opportunities for social activities. Stamp clubs and stamp shows exist in most mid-sized or larger cities—and where they do not exist, national, international, or internet-based societies stand by to provide services, assistance, information, and occasion for social interaction with other collectors. A collector has to decide what to collect, how much time and money to budget, what will maintain his or her interest over a long period of time, and how to display and enjoy the collection.

Learning about the stamps you have collected is enjoyable and gives you a greater appreciation of them. Once you begin you will find yourself completely enthralled with solving the mystery of who designed the stamp, what is illustrated on it, and where it is from.

## Purpose of This Book

*The Guide to Stamp Collecting* will lead a beginner through the steps of starting a stamp collection, proper care and handling of stamps, locating stamps for a collection, using the tools of a stamp collector, and deriving maximum enjoyment from a stamp collection. Don't worry about being confused by technical "collector jargon" and acronyms. Terms will be explained as they appear within the text, and a glossary of new terms appears at the end of the book.

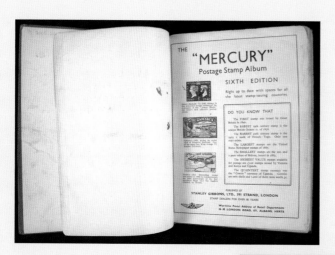

The title page of John Lennon's stamp collection onto which he drew beards and mustaches on Queen Victoria and King George VI. *From the Smithsonian National Postal Museum collection.*

# Dispelling the Myths

**Myth:** Stamp collectors are nerdy and obsessive about their collections.

**Truth:** Most collectors of anything are somewhat obsessive. Collecting is a passion. Stamp collectors are not any different in that regard. Stamp collectors are successful businessmen and women, sports stars, physicians, politicians, artists, actors, and lots of other smart, multi-

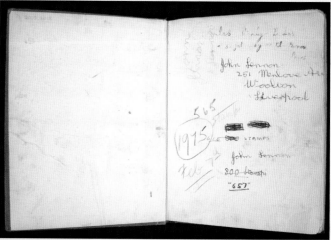

Rock 'n' roll singer/song-writer and former Beatle John Lennon collected stamps as a youth. His collection was acquired by the Smithsonian National Postal Museum in 2005. *From the Smithsonian National Postal Museum collection.*

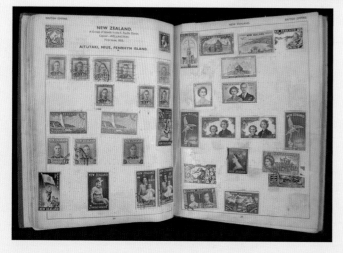

Pages from the Lennon collection containing stamps from New Zealand. *From the Smithsonian National Postal Museum collection.*

# About Stamp Collecting

faceted people just like you who enjoy the mental stimulation that stamp collecting provides. Singer/songwriter and former Beatle John Lennon collected stamps as a youth. President Franklin Roosevelt avidly collected stamps his whole life and Britain's King George V formed one of the world's greatest stamp collections, now owned and exhibited by Queen Elizabeth II. The late Prince Rainier of Monaco collected stamps. If you wanted to, you could form a sizeable collection of stamps bearing the portraits of famous people who also were stamp collectors.

Great Britain's King George V, shown on a British stamp issued in 1924, formed one of the greatest stamp collections of all time.

Stamp from the Principality of Monaco issued in 1947 showing President Franklin Delano Roosevelt working on his stamp collection.

The late Prince Rainier of Monaco, shown on this Monaco stamp from 1950, was a stamp collector.

### CHAPTER ONE

# THE STORY OF STAMPS

## From Queen Victoria to the King of Rock 'n' Roll

Postage stamps are everywhere. You use them to send letters and packages. You can buy them at the local post office or from a convenient vending machine. You receive them on your incoming mail. Maybe you glance at them occasionally before tossing them in the wastebasket. But where did these postage stamps come from? Why are they used? What do they do? How were they printed? The answers to those questions are traced back to the earliest days of written communication.

### The Earliest Postal Communications

The minute human beings began chiseling symbols into clay tablets they began to see the possibilities of written communication. Written messages could be saved and recorded. Couriers entrusted with messages did not have to try to remember them, and additional security could be applied depending upon the abilities of those seeing the message to read or decode it.

Biblical references to letter writing appear in the Old Testament, but the earliest postal services were established 3,500 years before that in China's Third Dynasty. A thousand years later, around 3000 B.C., organized posts were established in the Middle East.

OPPOSITE: Stamp detail. A ship in distress is illustrated in Art Deco style on this 1924 stamp from the Netherlands.

Persia (now Iran) issued stamps in 1915 that showed King Darius, who established a postal system in the fifth century B.C.

In the fifth century B.C., Greek historian Herodotus traced a system of courier relay stations, or post houses, that were established along the Royal Road during the reign of Darius of Persia. A messenger on horseback would stop at a station and pass the message on to another with a fresh horse. This ancient model spanned many centuries and was used by thousands of postal systems both large and small, including the famous Pony Express of the American Wild West.

Herodotus was the first postal historian. Among his writings was the now famous "Neither snow nor rain nor heat nor gloom of night stays these couriers from the swift completion of their appointed rounds" that graces the New York City Post Office building (now known as the Farley Post Office).

A more complex courier system known as Cursus Publicus developed in the Roman Empire during the time of Emperor Augustus. Its use was limited to official documents. Messengers used horses, chariots, and ships, relying on the technology of the day to speed the mail. Both Greeks

LEFT: This 1985 Austrian semi-postal shows a Roman courier on horseback. RIGHT: The ancient Roman mail system Cursus Publicus was illustrated on a stamp from Italy in 1976.

and Romans occasionally used homing pigeons to transport quickly small lightweight messages, making this the earliest form of aerial mail.

Although the postal network collapsed with the fall of the Roman Empire, monasteries and seminaries set up messaging systems throughout Europe during the Middle Ages —primarily because clergy constituted the largest literate population. As universities were established they became part of this communication network. Over time literacy became more commonplace, and courier services using horse-drawn carriages were utilized for government, commerce, and military purposes.

The Italian family of de Tour et Tassis (later Germanized to Thurn and Taxis) established Europe's most widespread postal system beginning in the late 1400s. Eventually this network of post offices extended from Italy to Germany, Austria, Hungary, Belgium, the Netherlands, Luxembourg, and Spain. Thurn and Taxis contracted with European royalty to carry official mail. Eventually ordinary citizens also could use the extensive Thurn and Taxis post, although sending or receiving letters was expensive. Remarkably, this private postal system lasted three and a half centuries, until 1867 when Prussia nationalized the last remaining Thurn and Taxis network.

Coaches, such as the Concord-style coach exhibited at the Smithsonian National Postal Museum, carried passengers and mail in North America. *From the Smithsonian National Postal Museum collection.*

An 1859 5-silbergroshen stamp from Thurn & Taxis Northern District. The Thurn & Taxis postal system was established by an Italian family in the late 1400s.

## Postal Reforms

The mid-eighteenth century ushered in the Industrial Revolution. By the late 1700s growing commerce created demand for better communication between suppliers, manufacturers, distributors, consumers, investors, and banks. Letters were written on sheets of vellum, parchment, or handmade rag paper and sealed with wax wafers or sealing wax. In many countries postage fees were calculated by the number of letter sheets and the distance the letter had to be carried.

In those days it was common practice for the recipient to pay the postal fees. This had the unfortunate consequence of adding significant expense to the delivery of mail. Frequently the recipient could not or would not pay the postage, which meant the postal service incurred all the cost of transporting a letter from one place to another without having been reimbursed for any of the costs of service.

In 1826 Rowland Hill, a former schoolteacher in Great Britain, became interested in methods to make the postal service more efficient. In his 1837 pamphlet *Post Office Reform: Its Importance and Practicability,* Hill recommended prepayment of postal fees with proof that the fees had been paid verified by use of prepaid letter sheets or a stamp, which he described as "a bit of paper just large enough to bear the stamps showing that tax had been paid, and covered at the back with a glutinous wash which the bringer of the letter might, by applying a little moisture, attach to the back." Hill further proposed that postal rates be set at 1 penny on every letter irrespective of the distance traveled within Britain, postulating that lower rates would increase volume, revenue, and efficiency.

Great Britain honored Rowland Hill with his own postage stamp in 1979. It was Hill who established postal reforms and "invented" the postage stamp.

Hill's plan did not receive unanimous acceptance, but it was eventually adopted by the British government in the British Postal Reform Act of 1839. Rowland Hill was appointed Advisor to the Treasury to implement the plan.

The British Treasury Department conducted a competition open to the general public to solicit designs for letter sheets and adhesive stamps. The competition generated more than 2,600 entries vying for the £200 prize for the most deserving, and £100 for runners-up—a very significant amount of money in those days. Most of the entries were for letter sheets and not adhesive stamps. Competition winners were selected and prize money paid, but none of the designs were adopted.

Rowland Hill believed **prepaid letter sheets** would be used to a far greater extent than adhesive stamps, the reason being that envelopes were not in general use at the time. Most letters were written on letter sheets, folded, and sealed with wax wafers. Stamp collectors call these **stampless letters** or **stampless entires.**

One of the period's most respected artists, William Mulready, was chosen to design the prepaid letter sheets. The adopted design shows a central figure of Britannia surrounded on both sides and down the left and right borders by a cast of characters that were intended to represent the entire vast British Empire.

A Mulready lettersheet used on the first day of issue, May 6, 1840. *Reproduced by the gracious permission of Her Majesty Queen Elizabeth II, to whom copyright belongs.*

## The World's First Stamp: The Queen Victoria Penny Black

The Treasury competition entries for adhesive stamps spanned a wide, creative interpretation of Rowland Hill's original vision of a "slip of paper . . . covered at the back with a glutinous wash." Top artists and printers of the day submitted incredible works of design and printing. Had any of them been adopted, our idea of what a postage stamp looks like could be very different.

Printer Charles Whiting proposed stamp designs, called **essays** by stamp collectors, which used two colors intricately woven together in ornate, engraved patterns not unlike the work done on banknotes. William Wyon, Chief Engraver of Seals to the Queen, submitted an essay using a profile of Queen Victoria that he had created for the Wyon City Medal in 1837. Wyon's profile, taken from a portrait of young Queen Victoria painted by Henry Corbould, became the basis for the adhesive stamp design that was eventually adopted.

The final design was created on commission by Henry Corbould. It drew inspiration from many of the Treasury Competition entries. Charles Whiting's ideas contributed the check letters at the bottom left and right corners of the stamp that proved conclusively each stamp's position on the printing plate. His ornately engraved essays inspired the engine-turned engraved background and side ornaments. The City Medal profile by

TOP RIGHT: A Penny Black, the world's first postage stamp. This is from the Plate 1 Imprimatur sheet dated April 18, 1840.
TOP LEFT: The Penny Black was released for use by postal customers on May 6, 1840. The illustration shows a Penny Black used on a folded letter mailed from Staunton (Great Britain) on June 6, 1840.
*Both images reproduced by the gracious permission of Her Majesty Queen Elizabeth II, to whom copyright belongs.*

An entry for the Treasury Competition for an unadopted "stamp" design called an "essay." This essay was created by Benjamin Cheverton in 1839. *Reproduced by the gracious permission of Her Majesty Queen Elizabeth II, to whom copyright belongs.*

William Wyon completed the amalgam that became the accepted design.

Rowland Hill engaged London printers Perkins, Bacon, and Petch for the task of engraving the die to create printing plates, making the plates, and then printing the stamps. A variety of proof printings and color trials were made. Finally, on May 1, 1840, the British Post Office released the world's first adhesive postage stamp for use by its customers. The stamp was printed in black ink upon paper that bore a watermark of a small crown. Each printed sheet contained 240 stamps that had to be cut apart with scissors. Each stamp featured a profile portrait of Queen Victoria. That stamp is still known today by its nickname: The **Penny Black**.

## Acceptance of Stamps, Lettersheets, and Penny Postage

Rowland Hill's postal reforms soon proved his ideas were right. The lower postal rates became known as "universal penny postage" and produced greater mail volume, increased revenue, and more efficient operation of postal services.

The idea of paying to mail a letter instead of making the recipient pay to receive it was met with initial misgiving by the public. Some believed pre-paying the fee would be insulting to the recipient, who might think the sender doubted his ability to pay for the postage upon delivery. Nevertheless, it did not take long for the public to appreciate the much lower postal fees and better service.

The Penny Black adhesive stamps were an instant hit with the public, but Mulready letter sheets were not. The elaborate design was mis-understood and ridiculed. Some even created cari-cature letter sheets mocking the Mulreadys. The Mulready letter sheets were withdrawn from public sale within a year, replaced by envelopes, which bore a printed and embossed design. Postal admin-istrations throughout the world continue to offer pre-stamped envelopes, postal cards, letter sheets, air letters, and other items of postal stationery for their customers. These objects are also eagerly sought by many stamp collectors.

## Emulating Success

Hill's slip of paper with a glutinous wash proved to be a great invention. Adhesive stamps were inex-pensive to produce and convenient to use. With most letters requiring a one-penny stamp, postal clerks no longer had to spend time figuring out the

## Where's it from?

Stamps bearing the portrait of Queen Victoria were issued in Great Britain until her death in 1901. These postage stamps established a pattern of British stamps featuring an image of the reigning monarch. Since Great Britain was the first country to issue stamps—and for a period of several years the *only* country to have postage stamps—the inscribed name of the issuing country was not deemed necessary. It still isn't, even though the Universal Postal Union, governing body for international postal affairs, declared in 1924 that postage stamps "shall, as far as possible, bear the name of the country of origin in Roman letters." Interestingly Great Britain was exempted from this regulation.

weight of the letter and the distance it would travel and calculating the postal fees based upon these measurements. The world's postal administrations took notice, but it would be a few years before other nations issued adhesive postage stamps. But by 1850, seven more countries were using stamps to signify prepayment of postage.

## 1843—Switzerland and Brazil

The country of Switzerland is made up of twenty-six cantons (similar to states in the U.S.). On March 1, 1843 the Swiss canton of Zurich issued postage stamps in 4 rappen and 6 rappen values. These numeral designs were printed by lithography in black ink on paper that had been printed with horizontal or vertical red lines. These lines served as an early form of security device.

The canton of Geneva issued sheetlets con-taining two 5 centimes stamps on September 30, 1843. The idea behind having two 5 centimes

First stamp of the Swiss canton of Zurich, released in 1843. *From the Smithsonian National Postal Museum collection.*

stamps sold together was the mailer could use them to send two letters for local delivery at 5-centimes each, or one letter to any destination within the canton for 10 centimes. These stamps were lithographed on yellow-green paper. Other Swiss cantons issued stamps of their own at later dates, but these were replaced in 1850 when Switzerland issued stamps for the entire confederation. Stamp collectors call these issues **Swiss Cantonals**. The two-stamp sheetlets from Geneva are known as **Double Genevas**.

On August 1, 1843, Brazil became the first country in the Americas to issue stamps. The design was a simple one of the numerals 30, 60, or 90 within a heavily ornamented oval. The stamps were printed from engraved plates on paper with either a gray or yellow tint. Because of their bold design within an oval, these first issues from Brazil acquired the nickname **Bullseyes**.

## 1847 — United States of America and Mauritius

The United States Post Office released its first two postage stamps July 1, 1847. The first was a 5 cents red brown on bluish paper that featured a portrait of Benjamin Franklin, the first Postmaster General of the United States. The second value was 10 cents (the stamp was inscribed with the Roman numeral X) and bore the portrait of George Washington, first President of the United States. That stamp was printed in black on bluish paper.

Mauritius, an island in the Indian Ocean off the coast of Africa, released its first issues on September 21, 1847. This

ABOVE: First stamp from Brazil, known as a "Bullseye," released in 1843. LEFT: First stamps from the United States. The 5 cent value shows Benjamin Franklin. RIGHT: The 10 cent value first issue of the United States depicts George Washington. *All three images from the Smithsonian National Postal Museum collection.*

colonial outpost of the British Empire used the Great Britain Penny Black as its model and gave the job of producing the stamps to James Barnard, a local jeweler, engraver and printer.

The first copper plate that Barnard produced had the word POSTAGE at the top, ONE PENNY or TWO PENCE at the bottom, POST OFFICE reading up the left side, and MAURITIUS reading up the right side of the stamp. The 1 penny stamp was printed in orange and the 2 pence in dark blue. Each stamp was painstakingly printed one at a time, unlike the Penny Black's sheet of 240 images printed at once. The first person to buy the Mauritius stamps the day they were placed on sale was the Governor's wife, who was preparing to send invitations to a ball she and her husband were hosting.

The following year the wording on the left side of the stamp was changed to POST PAID. The POST OFFICE Mauritius stamps never existed in large

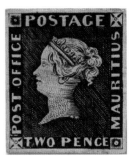

In 1847 the Indian Ocean island Mauritius issued two stamps, a 1 penny orange and a 2 pence dark blue, inscribed POST OFFICE instead of POST PAID. *Reproduced by the gracious permission of Her Majesty Queen Elizabeth II, to whom copyright belongs.*

quantity, and today rank among the rarest stamps in the world.

### 1849 — Bavaria, Belgium, and France

In 1849 Bavaria was an independent kingdom, although now it is a part of Germany. On November 1, 1849 the kingdom of Bavaria issued its first stamps in values of 1 kreuzer in black, 3 kreuzer (blue) and 6 kreuzer (brown). The stamps were square, printed by typography, and featured a prominent numeral for each value as the primary design element.

Belgium also issued its first stamps in 1849, consisting of two engraved values, a 10 cent in brown and a 20 cent in blue, bearing a portrait of King Leopold I.

The first French stamps were also issued that year. These stamps, printed by typography, illustrated the Roman goddess of agriculture Ceres, from which is derived the word "cereal." The Ceres design had a long run: France issued new Ceres values, with some design modifications, as late as the 1940s.

First stamp from Belgium, issued in 1849, showed Belgian King Leopold I. *From the Smithsonian National Postal Museum collection.*

# The Story Behind the Stamp

Each stamp holds a story beyond its ability to prepay for carrying mail. Unraveling those stories adds to the joy of collecting stamps.

Who was King Leopold I who appeared on Belgium's first stamp? Leopold was a prince of the German duchy of Saxe-Cobourg and Gotha. He served in the Russian Imperial Cavalry beginning with his appointment as colonel at the tender age of five. He became a general at age twelve, and at age twenty-five he was a lieutenant-general who had fought with honors against Napoleon.

In 1816 Leopold married Princess Charlotte Augusta of Wales, the sole legitimate daughter of the British Prince Regent (and future King George IV). Upon their marriage Leopold became a British field marshal and Knight of the Garter. Princess Charlotte died in childbirth in 1817. Had she lived, she would have become Queen of the United Kingdom and it would have been Charlotte's portrait on the world's first stamp instead of Victoria's.

Queen Victoria, daughter of Leopold's sister, Princess Victoria of Saxe-Cobourg, was Leopold's niece. He served as one of her advisors. Leopold accepted the appointment of "King of the Belgians" in 1831 after Belgium separated from the Netherlands and served in that capacity until his death in 1865.

## 1850s onward

More countries began issuing postage stamps and adopting postal reforms of their own. Some stamp collectors specialize in collecting the first stamps issued by every nation that has ever released postage stamps. Stamp collectors call this "First Issues" collecting.

Modifications to make postage stamps more convenient evolved quickly. Cutting the stamps apart with a scissors was laborious and time-consuming. In Great Britain Henry Archer invented a machine to punch a series of holes into sheets of stamps. These perforations made stamp separation quick and easy.

Stamps were made into booklets that could be carried safely in pocketbooks and wallets. They were also made into long coiled strips that were used in stamp vending machines. Businesses doing large mailings used coil stamps in stamp-affixing machines.

Over time, stamps became more sophisticated. The designs reflected the times in which they were issued, as well as new printing techniques that will be discussed in Chapter Two. The artistic styles changed and so did stamp designs. In the 1890s the heavily ornamented Victorian styles gave way to fluidly organic Art Nouveau. In the 1920s Art

LEFT: Victorian design was ornate and heavily ornamented, such as this 10 cent Washington stamp used in the United States from 1861 to 1872. *From the Smithsonian National Postal Museum collection.* RIGHT: An artistic style known as Art Nouveau can be seen on this 1916 newspaper stamp from Austria.

Nouveau was passé and Art Deco was the latest in stamp design. By the mid-1950s modern art took over. These stamps are characterized by clean, uncluttered type and little or no ornamentation. Stamps also became more colorful because new printing presses and techniques enabled stamp printers to do fast, economical multicolor printing.

At first the subjects illustrated on the stamps were heavily weighted toward reigning monarchs, national heroes, allegorical figures, and numerals indicating the amount of postage paid. Later stamps were used to commemorate important people and events, depict life and culture in the country of issue, and support commerce, tourism, and ideology.

Border disputes, wars, and treaties affected not only how mail traveled between nations but also the ultimate fate of nations. Some stamp-issuing countries ceased to exist when other nations invaded, or when a name change created a "new" country at the time of independence. Stamp collectors call such nations **Dead Countries**, and collecting postage stamps from countries that no longer exist is a very popular specialty for some collectors.

As stamps became more common, people began forming collections based upon the subject illustrated on the stamps. The world's postal administrations took notice and created even more colorful stamps showing popular subjects. On January 9, 1993, the U.S. Postal Service launched a series of stamps honoring American music by releasing a 29 cent stamp for Elvis Presley, the "King of Rock 'n' Roll." A year earlier the Postal Service had distributed ballots so the public could choose between two images for the stamp—a young 1950s Elvis or

**ELVIS PRESLEY – ROCK AND ROLL LEGEND**

**15TH ANNIVERSARY OF HIS DEATH**

The Caribbean island of St. Vincent released stamps to commemorate the King of Rock 'n' Roll, Elvis Presley.

an older 1970s "Vegas" Elvis. The voting was overwhelmingly in favor of the younger Elvis, whose image graces what is arguably the most popular United States stamp to date.

Stamp art and images have changed dramatically over time, but stamps themselves have not. How would you describe a postage stamp today? It would probably be something like this: a small rectangle of gummed paper upon which a design has been printed. If that description sounds a lot like Rowland Hill's conceptual description of a "slip of paper . . . covered at the back with a glutinous wash" it is because the idea still works well more than 170 years later.

### CHAPTER TWO

# BEGINNING A
# STAMP COLLECTION

## Get to Know Stamps

Some people are attracted by the flash of bright colors of a stamp on a letter. Others notice a favorite animal or scenic wonder illustrated on a stamp. Another person might see a stack of old letters in an antiques shop and become drawn to the thoughts and dreams of a writer from a century or more ago. Whatever the cause, once that magical attraction is recognized by an individual, stamps become more than just a method to pay postal fees.

### Stamp "Hardware"—Basic Parts of a Stamp

Stamps have practical elements that make them work. The paper, the watermark within the paper, the adhesive, the perforations, even the type of printing—all of these things serve a useful purpose and contribute to the functionality of a postage stamp in carrying a letter from one place to another. For stamp collectors, these elements also help identify and describe a stamp. In some cases, the difference of a watermark or gauge in the perforations might differentiate between a common stamp and a rare one.

OPPOSITE: Stamp detail. In 2001 Great Britain issued stamps illustrating weather conditions. The purple cloud at the bottom of the 27 pence stamp is printed with thermochromic ink that changes color when heated.

## Paper and Watermarks

Handmade paper starts its life as minutely chopped up wood, cotton, silk, linen, or some other natural fiber. Sometimes combinations of fibers are used. This material is mixed with water into slurry called **stuff**. Chemicals to brighten the paper, dyes to color the paper, colored silk or other fibers, and other agents may be added to the slurry that will affect the finished appearance of the paper. A screenlike mold is immersed into the stuff, and when it is withdrawn the solids stick to the screen and the liquid drains away. The solids are turned out from the mold onto felt to dry. This process is called **couching** the paper. When the couching is completed, the individual sheets of paper are removed and are ready for printing.

If paper is to have a watermark, the mold will have a pattern of thin wire attached to or incorporated into it. When the stuff adheres to the mold, the wire pattern will leave some areas of the paper thinner where the wires are, and where there are no wires the stuff will collect more thickly. Once the paper dries, the watermark will be visible if the paper is held up to a bright light. (Chapter Four discusses tools that are useful in finding and identifying watermarks on stamps).

The use of watermarks is a security measure. It makes counterfeiting a little more difficult because the paper has to have the right watermark to be genuine. This is why paper currency has such elaborate watermarks. Although they often cannot be seen from the face of the stamp, watermarks are nevertheless a vital part of it.

Today few stamps are printed on handmade paper. The entire process has become highly mechanized, with huge papermaking machines spewing out giant rolls of paper that are later fed into printing machines where the paper receives the stamp designs. Although this mass production results in continuous rolls of paper rather than individual sheets, the underlying process is still the same. Plant or wood fibers are made into a pulp with water. The stuff is disbursed across an enormous, continuous screen, which collects it and then drains the excess water away. If the paper is to have a watermark, it is at this stage that watermarking occurs.

The watermark pattern is either a part of the screen that collects the stuff, or a special roller called a "dandy," which carries the repeating raised design of the watermark. As the dandy rolls across the wet stuff, the watermark device slightly moves the fibers and microscopically changes the paper thickness at the watermark design. The screen itself may impart other characteristics that give different types of paper their names and special appearances.

From this point the paper is fed through a series of absorbent blanket rollers to complete the drying process and to press the paper into uniform thickness. Special coatings can be applied later, depending upon the requirements of the printing.

One coating that used to be applied to paper used for stamps was zinc white mixed with glue, which was sprayed on the surface of the paper. This prevented the printing ink from soaking into the paper fibers, so that if someone attempted to soak off a cancellation and reuse the stamp, the entire design would disappear too.

This coating was bad news for stamp collectors who want nice examples of used stamps for their

Sometimes during times of war and its aftermath, shortages of life's necessities occur. In post-World War I Latvia, paper was in short supply, so stamps were printed on the backs of old military maps.

collections, but it was an effective way for postal administrations to protect revenue.

There is special terminology to distinguish the main types of paper used to make stamps. Each collector needs to know the definitions of the various papers as they apply to what he collects, including wove, laid, chalky, granite, pelure, native, and goldbeater's skin.

The 1889 Imperial eagle with thunderbolts stamp from Russia was printed on laid paper.

## Most Common Paper Types for Stamp Printing

**Wove Paper** Flat, smooth paper with a slightly woven appearance resulting from the mesh of the screen made during the manufacture of the paper. Most current United States stamps are printed on wove paper.

**Laid Paper** Ribbed paper. The ribbing is caused from parallel screens used to gather the slurry-like stuff. The ribbing can be either horizontal or vertical and is described as such in catalog listings. When this ribbing is widely spaced, the paper is called **batonne.**

**India Paper** A thin, tough paper used mainly for printing proof impressions of stamp images from a die that will be used to manufacture the printing plate.

**Chalky Paper** Paper that has been given a coating of chalk before the stamp image is printed. Once the stamp has been used and receives a cancellation, should anyone attempt to remove the cancel, the image will come away from the paper with it. This is

This 1919 stamp from Austria shows the Parliament building. It was printed on granite paper.

a security device to prevent cleaning and reuse of the postage stamp. Chalky paper can be detected by touching a silver wire to it in an unobtrusive spot. The silver will leave a gray mark on chalky paper. Stamps printed on chalky paper should not be soaked to remove them from envelopes, as some or all of the image will be lifted.

**Granite Paper** Paper into which colored fibers have been added. This kind of paper is a deterrent to forgery because it is difficult to reproduce.

**Silk Paper** Paper that has had silk fibers added. Similar in appearance to granite paper.

**Pelure Paper** Thin paper that is strong and translucent, similar to onionskin paper.

**Native Paper** A very crudely handmade paper, usually containing large, visible fibers.

**Goldbeater's Skin** A very thin, translucent paper. Prussia printed stamps in reverse on goldbeater's skin in 1886 and then applied gum on top of the image. This was an extraordinary security measure

An 1875 4 cent proprietary revenue stamp from the United States was printed on silk paper.

This 1901 stamp from Russia was printed on pelure paper.

A Nepal stamp from 1899 was printed on crudely made native paper.

that made the stamps nearly impossible to remove from the envelope without loss of the image.

Stamps are generally printed in large **sheets** that can be subdivided into smaller, more manageable units called **panes**. Sheets and panes often have markings in the margins that are of interest to stamp collectors. These markings include plate numbers that identify the plate or plates from which the stamps were printed.

Printer imprints in margins can include logos, initials, or other markings that identify the printer of the stamps. Control markings are letters or numbers printed in the margins or sometimes even on the backs of stamps. These assist postal clerks in their accounting of the stamps.

Many other collectible inscriptions have been printed in stamp margins. In the United States this would include the cartoon figure of Mr. Zip encouraging the use of ZIP codes, "Mail Early in the Day" instructional inscriptions, arrows, electric-eye markings to guide perforators, registration markings, and initials of the siderographers, the individuals who created the plate from which the stamps were printed, to name but a few.

## Perforations and Methods of Stamp Separation

In 1840, when stamps were first developed in Great Britain, they were printed in sheets of 240 subjects. When customers wanted to buy some stamps, they would go to the post office and a postal clerk would cut the stamps off the sheet. This was time-consuming, and if the clerk was not careful, stamps were sold with parts of the design cut or missing.

It was not long before the problem of separating

Australia King George VI 2 ½ pence block of four stamps from 1950. The block has the imprint of the printer in the lower margin.

one stamp from another was tackled, most notably by Henry Archer of Great Britain. Small holes were punched into the margins between the stamps, making it easy for a postal clerk or customer to tear them apart. Those holes are called **perforations**, and perforations have a host of terms associated with them that describe their type, appearance, or measurements.

The different methods of making perforations are of interest to stamp collectors, and they can greatly affect the value of the stamps. **Comb**, **harrow**, and **line** are three basic types of perforations. These get their names from the patterns the perforating pins

make in the paper during the perforating process. Appearance of perforations might be described as **ragged** or **blind**, referring to perforation holes that were not cleanly cut. Or the stamps might be misperforated, where the perforations actually cut into part of the stamp design.

ABOVE: A block of twelve 2 pence stamps from the Gilbert and Ellice islands issued in 1956. The stamps were perforated by a comb machine. BELOW: A block of four 2 pence stamps from the Kingdom of Tonga issued in 1921. The stamps were perforated by a line machine. Notice that the holes do not meet squarely where they intersect.

Stamps with line perforations are those that have had their perforations made in a straight line, one or more rows of stamps at a time. For example, a sheet of stamps would have all the horizontal perforations applied and then be turned and have the vertical perforations done, one or more rows at a time. Stamps with line perforations often have holes that overlap one another where they intersect, thus giving the stamp corners an uneven appearance.

Stamps with comb perforations have at least three sides perforated at one time. Some comb machines completely perforate two or three rows and one row on three sides, then the sheet is advanced through the machine and the next row or rows have their perforations applied until the sheet is completely perforated. Stamps with comb perforations that have been perfectly applied have corner perforations that meet in alignment with no overlap.

Australia released this souvenir sheet showing pond animals in 1999. The sheet has harrow perforations and foil wings on the dragonfly that changes colors.

Sheets or panes of stamps that have been entirely perforated in a single operation are harrow perforated.

Problems can occur in the perforating process. Stamps can be misperforated, double-perforated, or not perforated at all. A machine that missed a row during the perforating process leaves a row or two of stamps with no perforations. Such stamps are listed in catalogs as "pair, imperf between," and are collected as imperforate-between pairs or blocks.

Blind perforations are slight indentations made by perforating pins, but there's no hole and no paper is missing. Punched-out perforation holes are called "chad."

The perforations on stamps can be measured, and the measurement of the perforations may be a deciding factor in determining a rare stamp from an otherwise identical-looking common stamp. Perforation gauges measure the number of holes or teeth per two centimeters. A stamp that measures "perf 11" is one that would have 11 teeth or 11 holes within the confines of two centimeters, if the stamp is that long. The gauge works for any stamp, no matter how large or small it is. (Instructions on how to use a perforation gauge are found in Chapter Four.)

Perforations that do not measure the same on all four sides of a stamp are known as "compound perforations." Catalogs list compound perforations by the horizontal (top and bottom) measurements first, followed by the vertical (side) measurements. Thus, a stamp listed as gauge 11 by 12 has top and bottom perforations that measure gauge 11 while the side perforations measure gauge 12. Some stamps have perforations that gauge differently on all four sides. Bosnia and Herzegovina's pictorial

Greece issued this "Tragedy of War" postal tax stamp in 1914. It has roulettes that were used to enable separation of one stamp from another.

definitives of 1906 are notorious for their multiple compound perforations.

Another method of stamp separation is called **roulette**. In stamp parlance, roulette has nothing to do with a spinning wheel in a casino. Instead of punching holes between the stamp designs, a rouletting machine applies a series of closely spaced cuts between them, allowing the stamps to be torn or pulled apart along the lines of the rouletting. Rouletting patterns include straight-line, arc, serrate, zig-zag, and serpentine.

Self-adhesive stamps that have wavy edges resembling perforations are actually die cut and not perforated at all. In the process of die cutting, blades will make "kiss cuts" around the stamp design that penetrate the stamp paper but not the

# The Story Behind the Stamp— Tonga's Banana Stamps

In the 1960s, British stamp innovator Bernard Mechanick introduced the first die-cut self-adhesive postage stamps to the world for the African nation of Sierra Leone and the Kingdom of Tonga in the South Pacific Ocean. In 1969 Tonga released stamps in the shape of one of their most important food sources and exports, bananas. The banana stamps were cut to shape and were sold in coiled rolls with peelable paper backing. They were very practical and were popular with island residents, who no longer had to concern themselves with keeping traditionally gummed and perforated stamps dry—a difficult task in the humid tropical climate. The banana stamps were followed by other self-adhesive stamps that had complex die-cut shapes such as Boy Scout tents, oil derricks, and military award ribbons. Stamp collectors disliked them because they were impossible to remove from envelopes so that they could be collected in albums, and because they did not look like other stamps. Mechanick was, however, twenty years ahead of the times. Today many of the world's postal administrations routinely issue stamps that are die-cut and self-adhesive.

The Kingdom of Tonga's revolutionary die cut self-adhesive banana-shaped stamps issued in 1969 were ahead of their time.

peelable backing paper to which the stamp is affixed. United States self-adhesive stamps usually have serpentine die cutting that mimics the effect of traditionally perforated stamps. Other countries have stamps that are ornately die cut into shapes.

## Adhesive—"Gum"

When Roland Hill wrote the description of his pre-paid postage adhesive, the postage stamp, he prescribed that it would be "covered at the back with a glutinous wash." Today that adhesive on the back of the stamp is called **gum** by stamp collectors. This is the part of the stamp that allows it to stick to the letter or parcel being mailed.

Gum that has to be wetted to be used is called water-activated. Gum that does not require wetting is called self-adhesive. The condition of the gum can dramatically affect the stamp's appearance and value to other collectors. (This will be discussed in Chapter Eight.) Gum also has characteristics not related to a stamp's condition, such as gum breakers. These are ridges that were impressed into the gum to help keep the stamps from curling.

Moisture-activated gum can be shiny or dull, depending on the formulation used.

There are also seasonal gums. In the past, hard gum tempered with gelatin was sometimes applied to stamps that were to be shipped and used in the warm summer months when the air has high moisture content. Soft, less moisture resistant gum is called winter gum.

Some stamps have printing on the gum side. This practice is called backprinting. If the printing is on top of the gum, it will be ruined or lost when the stamp is used.

## Types of Printing

Learning all about the different methods used to print stamps is part of a stamp collector's education. The technical aspects of printing include plate preparation, chemical processes, and different types of presses. For beginners, it is enough to learn how to tell one kind of stamp printing method from another. Some stamps that look alike are not the same because they have been printed by different methods.

### Intaglio, line engraving, engraving, recess printing

Great Britain's Penny Black was printed by a process called **line engraving** or **intaglio**, an Italian word meaning "incised" or "engraved." Intaglio printed stamps have crisp details. The ink is slightly raised above the surface of the paper, a quality that can be seen and felt. This form of printing is favored for banknotes and other security paper because it is more difficult to counterfeit.

### Photogravure, gravure printing

Photogravure is form of recess printing that uses a photographic process to transfer the stamp design to chemically treated metal—or more recently, plastic—printing plates, one plate for each color to

This 1937 stamp from French Equitorial Africa showing a raft on the Loeme River was printed by photogravure.

be printed. The process breaks the design into tiny dots, not unlike the dots of color you can find in a color illustration made by a computer inkjet printer. The dots can be seen easily with a magnifying glass. The finished printed surface is flat.

### Letterpress, typographic printing

Letterpress printing is the opposite of recess printing. The plate from which stamps are printed has a raised design rather than a recessed design. In appearance, the printed areas of letterpress printed stamps are slightly sunk into the paper. This characteristic is best observed on the reverse of the stamp.

LEFT: Cameroon, on the West coast of Africa, issued a series of engraved (intaglio) stamps showing magnificent African elephants in 1939. RIGHT: A 1917 1 centavo postage due from Mozambique was printed by typography.

The 1998 $2 butterfly stamp from Cook Islands was printed by lithography.

high-speed offset lithographic presses print most of the world's multicolored stamps.

### Embossing

Embossing is a process that raises the image above the paper surface, giving it a three-dimensional quality. The image may be without color—called "blind embossing" by stamp collectors—or have color added. Embossing is sometimes used on postage stamps but is more often found on items of postal stationery such as pre-stamped envelopes and postal cards.

### Lithography, surface printing, chromolithography, offset lithographic printing

Lithography or "stone lithography" is a chemical process that uses a flat polished stone, usually limestone, as the "plate" from which the image is printed. Stamps that have been printed by lithography are characterized by areas of solid, unbroken color.

Some nineteenth-century stamps were printed using traditional stone lithography, but the more common modern form of this type of printing is photolithography or offset lithography. Photolithography uses a photographic negative and a similar chemical process to apply the stamp images to a metal plate. Offset lithography transfers the image from the plate or cylinder to a rubber blanket that then transfers the image to paper. Today very

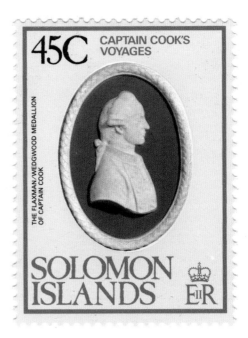

The head of Captain James Cook was embossed on this 1979 stamp from the Solomon Islands.

## Other Printing Formats

Holographic images have been used occasionally for stamps since 1988. The image is created on a plasticized metal foil. When light strikes the image it appears three-dimensional. Other types of foil have also been used for stamps. In 1963 the Kingdom of Tonga released a set of 13 stamps embossed on gold foil to commemorate Tonga's new gold coins.

More recently another innovation has found its way to postage stamp printing. Embroidered stamps have been issued by Switzerland. Stamps have been made from wood veneer. In 2001 Great Britain released a stamp that had an area printed with thermochromic ink that changes color at different temperatures. Advances in printing technology, coupled with great creativity, brought exciting changes to stamp designs.

A holographic image was added to a 1997 Aland souvenir sheet to commemorate the seventy-fifth anniversary of autonomy. A 1999 "peace dove" stamp from Canada is entirely holographic.

In 1964 the Kingdom of Tonga released a series of stamps to mark Polynesia's first gold coinage. The stamps were printed and embossed on gold foil.

## Luminescence

Modern stamps often have some form of luminescence that triggers automatic mail-sorting equipment. The equipment uses ultraviolet light that senses the luminescence on the stamp, triggering the "facing" of the envelopes so all of the address sides are face up and the postmarks go in the right place. For some stamps, the paper itself is luminescent, but for most, a phosphorescent coating is added to the face of the stamp. This is called **tagging**.

Tagging may be visible without special equipment, but it is usually only detectable with the help of shortwave or longwave ultraviolet light. Tagged stamps may have luminescent shapes, patterns, blocks, stripes, or overall coatings on them.

Austria produced the world's first embroidered stamp in 2000.

# Learn by Looking—Forming a Reference Collection

The fastest way to learn how to tell different types of printing is to assemble a reference collection using inexpensive stamps. Stamp catalogs will state how a stamp was printed, so collecting several different examples of each printing method and looking carefully at them will give you practical experience. Using stamps with the same design and seeing how the appearance changes by printing method is even more helpful.

An easy-to-acquire trio to begin a reference collection comes from Tasmania. Tasmania is now one of Australia's states, but at the time the stamps in question were issued Tasmania was a British colony. In December 1899 Tasmania released a set of eight stamps that illustrated Tasmanian scenery. In January 1902 the same designs in the same colors were printed by lithographic process and later that year they were again printed, this time by typography.

Let's use the 1 penny value for an exercise in creating a reference collection. Even though this stamp is over 100 years old, it is still commonly available and inexpensive, especially examples that have been used and bear a postmark.

The 1899 recess printing is easy to spot, because of the fine details and raised ink that is distinctive with this type of printing. Another good indicator is the watermark that can be seen on the reverse of the stamp. The recess printed stamps are the only ones with a watermark that has the letters "TAS" on a diagonal.

The 1902 lithographic stamps were printed on stamps bearing a watermark with a crown over the letter "V" or a "V" over a crown. The shading on the mountain in the background is almost nonexistent, giving the mountain a white appearance.

In October 1902 the stamps were printed by typography on "V" over crown watermarked paper. Heavy, coarse shading appears on the mountain and the path in the foreground, but it might be easier to

Tasmania released landscape stamps beginning in 1899. Many of the values, including this 1 penny, were printed three different ways: by engraving, typography, or lithography.

use one of the typographed examples from a September 1905 printing that was made on Crown over the letter "A" watermarked paper.

These are three similar stamps that are not the same. Learning to tell them apart will teach you about printing and watermarks.

## Stamp "Software" — Design Elements

The design elements of a stamp contribute to its appeal. Each element has a specific purpose and can either enhance or detract from the overall attractiveness of the stamp.

North Borneo is a former independent state and British protectorate that became a crown colony of the British Empire. (It is now a part of Malaysia called Sabah.) North Borneo issued many beautiful, eye-catching stamps. One of these, released in 1939, shows a proboscis monkey.

Look closely at this stamp. Notice that it was printed in two colors. The stamp would be called a **bi-color** by stamp collectors. The **frame** is purple and the central area of the design, called a **vignette** by stamp collectors, is olive green. The first element you see is almost certainly the monkey with his great, bulbous nose because the design elements were created to give star billing to the vignette.

The top of the stamp has the country of issue's name in English as well as the words POSTAGE and REVENUE. This portion of the stamp is called a **banner**, and the information contained therein tells you a lot about the country and the stamp. North Borneo is called a "state." The ribbon over the monkey's head contains the words "British Protectorate." This tells us that the stamp was issued prior to 1946 when North Borneo became a British crown colony.

The words POSTAGE and REVENUE tell us that the stamp did double duty. It could be used to pay postage fees for delivery of letters and parcels. It was also permissible to use the stamp to pay tax fees on documents such as deeds, duty on imported goods, and so on.

1939 North Borneo 4 cent proboscis monkey stamp, line engraved in purple and olive green, unwatermarked, with perforations that gauge 12 ½ on each side.

Moving down both sides of the stamp are words written in Malayan and Chinese. The bottom of the stamp has two boxes with the numeral 4 as well as a rectangle bearing the words FOUR CENTS. These indicate the amount or **denomination** of postal or revenue fees the stamp would have paid at the time it was in use. This area of the stamp is called the **value tablet.**

Stamp collectors would refer to this stamp by a catalog number (see Chapter Four for more about stamp catalogs) or by a lengthier process that states the country name, year of issue, denomination, subject, color(s), watermark (if any), and gauge of perforation.

This stamp is North Borneo, 1939 4 cent proboscis monkey line engraved in purple and olive green, unwatermarked, with perforations that gauge 12 ½ on each side.

Let's try the process on a later stamp with a more modern design, lacking the clearly defined frame, vignette, and value tablet areas of the North Borneo example.

France periodically issues stamps to honor French artists and their works. In 1970 French Impressionist artist Edgar Degas' painting *Ballerina* was featured on a 1 franc French stamp. The stamp has no value tablet, but the value is still a vis-

ible, if not prominent, part of the design at the bottom of the stamp. A blank area at the top of the stamp has the name of the country written in French "Republique Française" (French Republic). The frame is a very simple one containing no ornamentation that boxes in the main design and forms a banner containing the artist's name. This simpler style is less fussy, but the stamp still contains the basic elements of country name, denomination, and a central subject that focuses all the attention on Degas' beautiful art.

The stamp can be described as France, 1970 1 franc Degas' *Ballerina* painting, line engraved in multicolor, unwatermarked, with perforations that gauge 12 on the top and bottom and 13 on both sides.

As stamp printing and technology advances, stamp subjects and design have evolved to keep apace of the trends. Great Britain released a stamp with a very high face value of £10 in 1993. The stamp incorporates old and new technologies to minimize the possibility of forgery.

The paper upon which the stamp was printed is embedded with fluorescent threads that glow when exposed to ultraviolet light. The

1970 France 1 franc Degas' *Ballerina* painting, line engraved in multicolor, unwatermarked, with perforations that gauge 12 on the top and bottom and 13 on both sides.

1993 Great Britain £10 Britannia, combination multicolor printing by lithography, typography and embossed on granite paper, unwatermarked, with perforations that gauge 14 at top and bottom and 14 ½ on both sides.

design of Britannia was printed from engraved plates just as was the first Penny Black, but there is also **microprinting** that spells out TEN POUNDS in a repeating pattern at the bottom of the design. This is difficult to reproduce by xerography.

In addition to the fluorescent threads within the paper, the Union Jack emblem in Britannia's shield glows bright yellow and another fluorescent area reads TEN POUNDS in blue when subjected to ultraviolet light. The silhouette of the Queen is in a silver metallic ink, there are elliptical security perforations at the top of each stamp and, for good measure, the number TEN is embossed in Braille on the stamp.

This fascinating stamp is described as Great Britain, 1993 £10 Britannia, combination multicolor printing by lithography, typography, and embossed on granite paper, unwatermarked, with perforations that gauge 14 at top and bottom and 14 ½ on both sides.

Chapter Four will describe how, with the use of a stamp catalog, a complicated description of a stamp can be whittled down to a catalog number that can be used when ordering stamps from a dealer.

### CHAPTER THREE

# WHAT TO COLLECT

## Types of Stamps

When postal administrations make more options available to the public they often create special stamps to pay for the services to be rendered. Parcel post, special delivery, and airmail are among the additional services that have their own stamps. The world of stamp collecting embraces all of the many types of stamps.

### Regular Issues, Definitive Stamps

The terms **regular issues** and **definitives** are used interchangeably for stamps used on ordinary mail and parcels. Regular issue stamps are released by postal administrations for indefinite, but usually extended periods of use. In the United States, regular issue stamps are normally small in size and commonly illustrate an American flag. These are the stamps seen on most day-to-day mail. Other countries use larger sizes for their regular issues, but they are still used for extended periods of time and are the workhorse stamps used for the majority of business and private correspondence.

Most beginners will acquire large quantities of regular issue stamps collected from their own mail and from buying inexpensive mixtures. Having so many stamps that look the same

OPPOSITE: Stock books are excellent for storing stamps.

AUSTRALIA
Tenpin-bowling
2c

A definitive stamp from Australia released in 1989. This series showed different kinds of sports enjoyed by Australians, including bowling shown on this 2 cent stamp.

An inverted center is a spectacular error. This 4 cent inverted center was released in 1901 for the Pan American Exposition and illustrates an electric automobile. *From the Smithsonian National Postal Museum collection.*

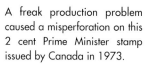

anada 2 C

A freak production problem caused a misperforation on this 2 cent Prime Minister stamp issued by Canada in 1973.

at first glance can lead a beginner to select just one stamp for their collection and cast aside the remainder. This is almost always a bad idea. Because regular issue stamps are used for long periods of time, it is highly likely there will be several printings of the stamps. Multiple printings frequently result in changes in colors, perforations, gum, paper, tagging, microprinting, or watermarks. For the sake of customer convenience, postal administrations release regular issue stamps in a variety of formats that include

booklets that fit into wallets or handbags and coiled rolls of 100 or more. These added formats are also collectable.

Consult a stamp catalog and review the listings for any regular issue stamp to see if more than one entry exists for it. (Instruction on how to use a catalog is found in Chapter Four.) A specialized catalog might also go into additional details and list **errors** such as missing colors, **freaks** such as misperforations, and other **varieties** that may have occurred during production.

ABOVE: A printing plate variety caused the top of the crown on this Australian stamp to be cut off. A normal example shown for comparison. LEFT: A definitive or regular issue stamp issued in 1923 by the United States. This 14 cent stamp features a vignette portrait of an American Indian. *From the Smithsonian National Postal Museum collection.* RIGHT: A large pictorial definitive stamp released by South Pacific island nation Aitutaki in 1984.

Utgivningsdag: 25 november 1986
Förlagor: Ingalill Axelsson
Gravör: Martin Mörck
Omslag: Jan Magnusson

## Commemorative Stamps

Commemorative stamps are issued specifically to honor a person, place, thing, historic anniversary, or event. Some commemoratives focus attention on programs such as conservation, or on social issues. Commemorative stamps are usually issued for a limited period of time before they are withdrawn from sale. Often commemorative stamps are larger in size than regular issues. Their bright colors, attractive designs, and interesting subject matter make them popular with both stamp collectors and the general public.

ABOVE RIGHT: The United States first issued commemorative stamps in 1893 for the World's Columbian Exposition held in Chicago. The 1 cent is shown here. *From the Smithsonian National Postal Museum collection.* LEFT: Commemorative stamps have also been released in booklet format. This, from Sweden in 1986, shows Nobel Peace Prize Laureates including Martin Luther King Jr. and Mother Teresa. RIGHT: Commemorative stamps can be issued in multi-design formats called souvenir sheets, such as this example showing movie star Marilyn Monroe issued by St. Vincent in 1995.

# Pick a Card . . . Any Card!

Do you enjoy playing poker or pinochle? Deal a few stamps with playing cards into your collection. No matter what your interest, the odds are in your favor that it has been illustrated on a stamp. Toys, gemstones, boats, paintings, trains, dogs, cats, and animals of all sorts appear on thousands of stamps from all over the world. Collecting stamps by the subject matter illustrated upon them is called **topical** or **thematic** collecting. Pick a subject . . . any subject . . . and you will find stamps to match.

Playing cards illustrated on German Democratic Republic stamps from 1967. Collecting stamps by the subject shown on the stamps is called topical or thematic collecting.

An airmail stamp from Greece issued in 1926 shows a flying boat as seen through a colonnade.

## Airmail Stamps

Airmail stamps are used to pay the fees for airmail service in transporting a letter or parcel. Airmail stamps are perhaps the best known and most ubiquitous of the special service postage stamps.

When airplanes began carrying mail there was usually an added fee for this expedited service. Today many countries, including the United States, are phasing out airmail stamps for domestic use, but still occasionally issue special stamps for international airmail.

## Precancels

Precancels are stamps that have had a cancel printed or handstamped prior to their sale and use. This is done primarily for stamps that will be used for bulk mailings so that the post office need not individually postmark the stamps.

A precancel from Hartford, Connecticut on a United States 1¼ cent Santa Fe regular issue stamp.

## Perfins

Perfin is a term that is a combination of two words: perforations and initials. A perfin, therefore, is a stamp on which initials, or less commonly some other design, have been perforated into the stamp's design area. This is done as a form of security for businesses or government departments to prevent employees from using these stamps for their own private mail.

A 50 mark official stamp from Germany, issued in 1922.

Perforated initials, or "perfins" that read BENY (Board of Education New York) on a United States 8 cent Liberty stamp.

## Official Stamps

Many countries issue official stamps for use on correspondence sent by authorized government departments and agencies. These stamps may be specially designed for official mail, but often they are ordinary postage stamps overprinted or punched with initials (perfins) to signify their special purpose. Official stamps often bear the words OFFICIAL, SERVICE, DIENSTMARK, or the initials O.S. (Official Service) or OHMS (On Her/His Majesty's Service).

A 1978 Cook Islands stamp overprinted O.H.M.S. and surcharged 35 cents in silver ink. The O.H.M.S. initials mean ON HER MAJESTY'S SERVICE and could only be used on official mail.

## Postage Dues

Postage dues are used on letters and parcels that have had insufficient postage affixed. The recipient is required to pay the amount of the shortage that is indicated by postage due stamps. Many stamp collectors prefer to collect postage dues "affixed to the envelope" to illustrate the postal rate that should have been paid originally and the amount of the shortage that was paid by the recipient upon delivery.

A postage due stamp, issued in triangular format, from Nyassa (now a part of Mozambique) in 1924.

## Semi-Postal Stamps

Semi-postal stamps carry with them an additional fee over and above that collected for postal services. The extra fee collected in this manner is given to a designated charity. The purchase and use of semi-postal stamps is voluntary.

The United States issued its first semipostal, the **nondenominated** (not having a face value printed on the stamp) Breast Cancer Research stamp, in 1998. As of this writing the extra fee on the Breast Cancer Research stamp has generated nearly $50 million to benefit research for breast cancer.

Some unusual charities have benefited from funds raised by the sale of semi-postal stamps. Between 1935 and 1940 France issued semi-postal stamps to support unemployed intellectuals. Prisoners of war, famine relief, restoration of cathedral windows, and refugee relief have all received money acquired from the sale of semi-postal stamps.

## Postal Tax Stamps

Governments sometimes mandate a tax on letters and parcels. This postal tax may be collected for a variety of reasons, but unlike a semi-postal stamp that collects a voluntary extra fee, a postal tax is obligatory. The tax must be paid in order to send a letter or parcel and affixing a postal tax stamp to the mail piece indicates that the tax has been paid.

India, faced with the care of millions of refugees fleeing ethnic violence in Bangladesh in 1971, printed the words REFUGEE RELIEF on then current stamps illustrating the theme "Family Planning." This stamp became a receipt for the compulsory tax on all letters to support humane care of the Bangladeshi refugees.

LEFT: In 1980 Finland released stamps showing a popular collecting topic of mushrooms. The stamps raised money to benefit the Red Cross. RIGHT: In 1971 India imposed a compulsory tax on letters to provide funds that would aid refugees from Bangladesh.

## War Tax Stamps

Many nations needing additional revenue to pay for armed conflicts have imposed taxes of various kinds on their citizens, including taxes on mail. The money collected is not part of a postal rate because the post office does not keep the extra money. Rather, the tax collected by the post office goes into government funds to help pay for the costs of fighting a war.

During World War I the United States instituted a tax of one cent for first-class letters that went into effect November 2, 1917 and remained in effect until June 30, 1919. The tax was paid by the use of ordinary postage stamps, and no special war tax stamps were issued by the United States.

Other countries also had obligatory taxes on the mail and issued war tax stamps specifically for the payment of this tax. Sometimes the stamps were especially designed and printed; other countries simply overprinted WAR TAX on ordinary postage stamps.

## Parcel Post Stamps

Parcel post stamps are used to pay a reduced rate for qualifying parcels. Some countries, Italy among them, issued parcel post stamps in two parts divided by perforations. Half of the pair is affixed to the parcel, with the sender retaining the remaining half as a receipt.

Parcel post stamps are frequently difficult to find used on their original packaging because most parcels are opened and discarded. The U.S. Parcel Post stamps issued in 1912 are attractive and illustrate mail delivery methods and the industries that would have used them, but they were only used a relatively short period of time.

ABOVE LEFT: A 1 cent war tax overprint on a stamp from Antigua. The stamp was issued in 1918 to pay a compulsory tax on letters that would help pay costs of World War I. ABOVE RIGHT: United States Parcel Post stamp issued in 1912 for sending parcels at a reduced rate. The 2 cent stamp illustrates a city mail carrier delivering mail door to door. BOTTOM RIGHT: The Parcel Post service was sometimes used to carry unusual items, such as this parcel that contained a queen honeybee. *From the Smithsonian National Postal Museum collection.*

## Registered Letter Stamps and Certified Mail Stamps

Registered mail is an added-fee service for sending a letter or parcel in a secure way and carries compensation if a mail piece becomes lost or damaged. Each letter or package sent by registered mail receives a unique number. The sender receives a receipt bearing this number. The registered mail piece is recorded and usually receives a transit marking at each point along the route of delivery, enabling each registered letter to be tracked. The recipient is required to sign a receipt upon delivery. Some countries issued stamps for the registration fees.

Certified mail is similar to registration in that it is a secure method to send letters or parcels with a receipt for proof of mailing and delivery, but carries no compensation for loss or damage.

A 1924 registration stamp from Liberia paid the added fee for registering a letter.

United States 20 cent special delivery stamp from 1925. The stamp shows a post office truck.

## Special Delivery Stamps

Special delivery is an added-fee expedited service that required immediate delivery of a letter or parcel upon arrival at the destination post office. Such mail did not have to wait for the next regular delivery.

The United States issued the world's first special delivery stamp on Oct. 1, 1885. That service has now been phased out in the United States and replaced by the more efficient (and much more expensive) Express Mail. U.S. special delivery stamps paid only for the extra fee for this special service and were used in tandem with regular postage stamps to pay the postal rates in effect at the time. Special delivery stamps have also been issued by Canada, Mauritius, New Zealand, Bulgaria, and many Spanish-speaking nations.

## Express Mail Stamps

Express Mail is a service available in the United States that uses special purpose stamps. This service, which began in the 1970s, guarantees next day delivery for most addresses. The stamps, first issued in 1983, are usually colorful and oversized. These stamps can be used on other types of mail, although they are seldom seen other than in collector hands. Many post offices do not stock them but instead use postage-value-indicated (PVI) meter strips.

Other countries have express mail stamps and services that predate Express Mail in the United States. Italy, for example, issued stamps in 1902 inscribed ESPRESSO, but these were used for special delivery rather than guaranteed overnight delivery services.

## Newspaper Stamps

Many countries established preferential reduced postal rates for newspaper delivery because dissemination of news and opinion was beneficial to the commerce and development of a nation. With the reduced rates came special stamps to pre-pay the rates.

Newspaper stamps had varied uses. Some were used on individual newspapers, some were used on bundles of newspapers, and some were used on receipts. Austria was the first country to issue newspaper stamps. These were nondenominated, and the color of the stamp indicated its postal value. Many other countries issued interesting and highly collectible stamps expressly for the carriage of newspapers, and fortunately a great many fall within easy reach of very modest stamp budgets.

Closely related to newspaper stamps are newspaper wrappers, sheets of paper that bear an imprinted stamp that are wrapped around a newspaper with the stamp imprint and the address on the outside. The wrapper was secured with its own gummed flap or with a label or a seal. Wrappers are collected as entires—that is, the complete wrapper should remain intact.

LEFT: A 1920 10 filler newspaper stamp from Hungary. ABOVE: Newspaper wrapper from the colony of Victoria, now a part of federated Australia. The wrapper held an edition of *Bendigo Advertiser* mailed from Bendigo in January 1897.

## Telegraph Stamps

Telegraph stamps were those used to prepay the fees for sending a telegram. In some countries the telegraph system came under control of the post office. In others, such as the United States, telegraph services were privately owned and operated, but both private and government-operated services were known to use stamps.

A telegraph stamp released in the United States by the Northern Mutual Telegraph Company in 1883.

## Revenue Stamps

Revenue stamps are those with no postal function that are used to indicate payment of a wide variety of taxes. Revenue stamps are commonly used for taxes that may be incurred when cashing bank checks, transferring stock, registering a deed, executing a will, creating a bill of lading, or paying hundreds of other taxes imposed by government agencies. A vast number of revenue stamps exist from nearly every country in the world. Collecting them is a popular branch of stamp collecting.

An Australia 2 shilling stamp overprinted for use by Australian military occupying Japan at the end of World War II. The B.C.O.F. initials mean BRITISH COMMONWEALTH OCCUPATION FORCE.

## Military Stamps

Military stamps are used by active service personnel under a variety of circumstances, usually as part of a fighting force in war time or as part of an occupation force. Military personnel frequently receive reduced or "concessionary" postal rates and the denominations of the stamps reflect these rates.

An Australian 2/- dark red-brown Kangaroo and Map definitive stamp overprinted B.C.O.F. JAPAN 1946 is shown above. These stamps were used by Australian military personnel serving with the British Commonwealth Occupation Force in Japan after World War II.

A $2 United States revenue stamp issued in 1871 for the Internal Revenue Service.

## Postal Fiscal Stamps

Postal fiscal stamps can be used for a broad category of services. They straddle the line between postage and revenue stamps. Postage stamps pay for postal services, while fiscal stamps pay for fees and taxes for other kinds of governmental services such as deed or stock transfers, taxes on imported goods, and licensing and inspection fees. Postal fiscal stamps do both.

New Zealand 9 shillings postal fiscal stamp issued in 1948. The stamp could be used for postal or revenue purposes.

Mint postal-fiscal stamps and those that have been used on letters or parcels are of interest to postage stamp collectors because they could be or were used to pay for postal services. Stamp catalog values for used postal-fiscal stamps are for those that were used postally. That does not mean that fiscally used stamps are not collectible, just that they are generally less valuable than postally used stamps. Revenue stamp collectors may collect fiscally used postal-fiscal stamps in their own right without regard to postal usage.

## Surcharges and Overprints

A **surcharge** is specifically related to the face value of a stamp. For example, if there is a postal rate increase, some countries choose to revalue a stamp of a different denomination by printing a new value on the top of or adjacent to the old value (see Provisional Stamps in this chapter).

Stamps can also be surcharged for charitable purposes, converting ordinary postage stamps into semi-postals.

An **overprint** is any printing that is added on top of a stamp. It can take many forms and serve numerous purposes. Ordinary postage stamps have been overprinted AIRMAIL, thus converting the stamps into ones that could only be used to send letters and parcels by airmail. The word OFFICIAL has been overprinted on stamps, which limited the use of the stamps for government mail only.

Another reason stamps are overprinted is to signify a political change in the country of issue. Some countries came under administration by British military just after World War II. Postage stamps were overprinted BMA. The initials stand for "British Military Administration," and reflect the interim British military government after liberation from Japanese occupation.

LEFT: 1945 BMA overprint on a Straits Settlements stamp issued for the British Military Administration of Malaya at the end of World War II. BELOW: Sierra Leone surcharged a 2 pence stamp with a new decimal currency value of 5 cents in 1965.

LEFT: A 1 penny Great Britain King Edward VIII stamp was overprinted TANGIER for use in the international zone of Tangier in Morocco.

RIGHT: In 1928 the United States overprinted 2 cent regular issue stamps MOLLY PITCHER to commemorate the Battle of Monmouth. *From the Smithsonian National Postal Museum collection.*

Overprints are sometimes added to stamps from one country for use in another country.

The British 1 penny King Edward VIII stamp shown above was overprinted for use in the Tangier international zone. This stamp is found in the *Scott Catalogue* at the back of the listings for Great Britain Offices in Morocco. It is Scott 512.

Stamps may also be overprinted for commemorative purposes. The United States overprinted a 2 cent carmine George Washington definitive in 1928 with the words MOLLY PITCHER to commemorate the 150th anniversary of the Battle of Monmouth. Molly Pitcher was a name acquired by Mary Hays, who assisted Continental soldiers in the battle by dodging bullets to bring them pitchers of cool water.

The words *surcharge* and *overprint* are often used interchangeably by stamp collectors. In reality, all surcharges are overprints, but not all overprints are surcharges. Surcharges and overprints are prone to forgery because it is less trouble to apply a bogus overprint to a genuine stamp than it is to produce an entirely counterfeit stamp. Before spending a lot of money for a valuable overprinted stamp, it is wise to acquire a certificate of genuineness from a recognized expertization service. (See Chapter Eight, "Getting an expert's opinion.")

## Provisional Stamps

Provisional stamps came into being to fill a short-term need or requirement. They can take many different forms. Probably the most recognizable provisionals are those that have been surcharged.

Surcharging is most often caused by a postal rate change, which requires stamps with new denominations be produced quickly. Existing stamps are overprinted with a new denomination. Usually the old value is obliterated, either by the new value itself or by bars or other devices. Stamps can be surcharged and placed into use very rapidly. They generally remain in use until stamps with proper denominations meeting the new postal rates can be printed and distributed to post offices.

Not all rate-change provisionals are surcharges. The United States has issued provisional stamps without any denomination, or with only a letter indicating that the stamp was good for domestic letter-rate postage. These stamps were printed well in

The French colony of Martinique, a Caribbean island, surcharged a 1 franc stamp, uprating it to 1.25 francs in 1926. This is a provisional stamp.

Great Britain stamp inscribed "2nd" for second-class letters within Britain, originally sold at post offices for 20 pence. It remains valid for second-class letters "forever," regardless the rate at time of use.

advance of any postal rate increase. Since it was not known far enough in advance what rate would be approved, nondenominated stamps could be printed far ahead of the need. But nondenominated stamps create a problem. At the time nondenominated stamps are issued, almost everyone knows what values they represent. Over time, it becomes a little fuzzy what the face value was meant to be. Some countries, such as Great Britain, have begun issuing nondenominated stamps inscribed to pay the fees for particular classes of mail. The stamps are sold by the post office at the prevailing rate and will satisfy the payment for sending the specified class of mail indefinitely regardless of future postal rate increases. For this reason, the stamps are called **forever stamps.**

Stamp shortages account for many provisional issues. Stamp shortages have been caused by interruption of supplies, stamp theft, damage by flood or fire, and other equally unpredictable reasons. Natural disasters have created shortages as well. Storms, earthquakes, tidal waves, and volcanic eruption have all affected post offices somewhere at some time. Sometimes postmasters had to get creative to be able to provide stamps for their customers, going so far as to cutting stamps of higher value in half and using them for half of their face value to cover a common postal rate for which no stamps were available.

Periods of rapid inflation cause havoc everywhere, but especially for postal administrations. In Germany during the 1920s, hyperinflation escalated prices of everything to the degree that workers were being paid twice a day and carried their worthless wages in shopping bags and wheelbarrows. At the beginning of 1923, it cost twenty-five marks to mail a letter from one city in Germany to another. By the end of 1923, after sixteen rate changes, it cost 100 trillion marks to mail the same letter. There were five rate changes in the

A provisional stamp from Germany in 1923 when there was hyperinflation. The stamp was surcharged and uprated from 5 marks to 2 million marks.

month of November 1923 alone, going from 100 million marks on November 1 to 80 trillion marks on November 30. Printing new surcharges on stamps to keep up with the rate changes became a major challenge.

Italy was occupied by Austria in 1918. Austrian military stamps were surcharged in Italian currency and used in occupied Italy.

## Occupation Stamps

War has a way of changing governments rapidly, resulting in another type of provisional stamps used in countries occupied by others. One of the quickest ways to produce occupation stamps is to overprint either the stamps of the country being occupied or the stamps of the occupying country, so a sizeable percentage of all occupation stamps ever issued have been provisional stamps.

## Local Stamps

Local stamps are for use in a specific region or a limited postal system. Locals may be officially issued by postal authorities or unofficially issued by private carriers or corporations. Local stamps are usually not valid for national or international delivery.

In the middle of the nineteenth century, local posts thrived in the United States. Private city delivery and express services issued adhesive stamps for use on letters and packages. One of these local posts was the famous Wells Fargo Pony Express. There were also many city dispatch postal services.

Local delivery systems have sprung up when mail carriers have gone on strike. In 1971, postal workers in Great Britain went on strike. Within days, hundreds of local posts began operation, many of which issued their own stamps.

In addition to private delivery services, there are many other types of local stamps. Both Australia and New Zealand have stamps issued in the names of their Antarctic research bases. Unlike true local stamps, however, these stamps are good for prepayment of postage for mail delivery both nationally and internationally.

### Common Designs—Joint Issues, Key Plates, and Omnibus Stamps

Occasionally two or more postal administrations get together and issue stamps with identical or similar designs to commemorate a person or event of common interest. These stamps, issued on the same day or within a few days, are called **joint issues**.

Stamps issued for research bases in the Australian Antarctic Territory are considered to be local stamps by some stamp catalog publishers.

## German Occupation of Alsace

The ELSAß overprinted 50 pfennig green and gray Hindenburg stamp shown here is a provisional occupation stamp. The stamp was issued in 1940 during the German occupation of Alsace after the fall of France. Alsace was part of the Holy Roman Empire and was annexed by France in 1697. The people spoke a Low German dialect. In 1871 with the unification of Germany, Alsace became part of the German province of Elsass and Lothringen. In 1919, Alsace was returned to France.

The occupation stamps were in use for only a short period of time in 1940, until Alsace was incorporated into Germany as part of the Baden-Elsass district. From that point on, German stamps were used. Alsace was returned to France in 1945.

Germany occupied the Alsace region of France during World War II. In 1940 German von Hindenburg stamps were overprinted Elsaß, "Alsace" in German.

LEFT: The United States's first joint issue was with Canada. Both stamps had the same design and marked the opening of the St. Lawrence Seaway in 1959. RIGHT: A 1949 "key plate" stamp from Leeward Islands. An image of the King was on one printing plate. A second plate contained the country's name and denomination in local currency.

The United States first ventured into the realm of joint issues in 1959 with the 4 cent St. Lawrence Seaway stamp issued to commemorate the opening of the Seaway. Canada was the U.S. partner and issued a nearly identical stamp for the cooperative project. In the years since, the United States has collaborated with more than twenty different nations, some of them more than once, to issue common-design postage stamps.

But joint issues are not a modern concept. In fact, **key plate stamps** or **keytype stamps** can be considered forerunners of the more recent joint issues. Key plate is a stamp term that is applied to a wide range of postage stamps issued by some British, Portuguese, German, and French colonies. The design of a stamp was a generic portrait of the reigning monarch or other image. There was a blank tablet for the country name and another blank for the stamp's denomination.

The basic design could be printed in quantity and used indiscriminately for any of the participating colonies. The plate that printed the basic design was called a "key plate." Later the country's name and the proper denomination were added using printing plates created for that specific purpose. Those printing plates were called "duty plates."

This method was cost effective. Creating new designs and plates from which they could be printed was an expense many of the smaller colonies simply could not afford. The key plates allowed even the smallest, most disadvantaged countries to have their own postage stamps.

Omnibus stamps are those released in matching or similar designs by multiple countries to commemorate the same person or event.

A popular collecting topic, Europa stamps have been issued nearly every year by an increasing number of countries since 1956 to symbolize cooperation among European nations.

This one-size-fits-all design concept made a natural transition to **omnibus issues** released by Portugal, Great Britain, and some other countries. An omnibus is issued by several postal entities to note a common theme. The stamps may have the same design, but it is not required.

In 1956, six European nations issued a stamp with a common Europa design. The Europa theme has been ongoing, with an ever-increasing number of countries participating by issuing a common design or unique designs focusing on the theme of Europa.

### Personalized Stamps

New on the scene are personalized stamps that are created with a picture supplied by the purchaser. Some countries' postal services, such as Australia, China, and Great Britain, issue stamps with a blank tab onto which the desired personalized photograph is printed. The stamp and label together are affixed to envelopes. In the United States, the customer-supplied

image is printed directly on a "stamp" that is more properly called a postage meter label. These kinds of "personalized stamps" are the product of private firms who have been approved by the United States Postal Service to produce and distribute them. All personalized stamps are sold at a premium over and above the face value of the stamps.

### Stamp Formats

Postage stamps are available in a variety of formats designed for the postal customer's convenience. The most familiar format is in a **sheet** or a **pane**. Stamp collectors refer to a sheet as the unit that comes off the printing press. Quite often these contain hundreds of stamps and are very large and unwieldy. These large sheets are difficult for postal clerks to handle and so before distribution to post offices they are cut into smaller units called panes. Most of the time when a postal customer goes to a post office and asks for a sheet of stamps, it is really a pane

LEFT: A United States personalized stamp produced for the author and her husband by stamps.com. RIGHT: A pane of stamps from Palau commemorate the United States–Palau postal agreement.

LEFT: A coil pair of Australian 5 cent Queen Elizabeth II regular issue stamps of 1967. RIGHT: A souvenir sheet from India, released in 2000, featuring gems and jewelry.

of twenty, forty, fifty, or one hundred stamps that will be sold to the customer.

**Coil stamps** are those made into coiled rolls. They were created with the advent of machines that would vend postage stamps and other machines that would affix stamps to envelopes for mass mailing. Jumbo coil rolls of 10,000 stamps fit into this kind of machinery, but the ordinary postal customer can order coils in more manageable rolls of one hundred.

**Stamp booklets** are a convenience for postal customers. Originally sheets of stamps were cut into much smaller units that were stitched or stapled together with paper covers. Sometimes interleaving was added to keep the water-activated gum from sticking together in high humidity. The stamp booklets fit into wallets and handbags, making them enormously popular with mailers. Most stamp booklets produced in the United States these days are "convertible stamp booklets." They

are purchased as a double-sided sheet of self-adhesive stamps. The sheet can be folded into thirds without damaging any of the stamps, making a tight package that fits easily into a wallet.

Great Britain issued a new form of booklet in 1969 that had added interleaving pages with text and color illustrations. The booklet from 1969 is called "Stamps for Cooks" and contains recipes and illustrations of the prepared dishes. Now Great Britain and other countries routinely issue this form of booklet focusing on a variety of popular subject matter. They have become known as **prestige booklets**.

**Souvenir sheets** are sometimes called **miniature sheets**. They are usually commemorative. They contain one or more stamps related to a specific theme along with decorative elements printed in the margins outside the stamp area. The decorative elements have no postal validity.

A 1990 stamp booklet from Australia features paintings.

A butterfly-shaped souvenir sheet from Pitcairn Island, released in 2005.

Great Britain memorialized Princess Diana with a set of five se-tenant (joined together) stamps in 1998.

**Se-tenant** is a French term that means *joined together*. Se-tenant stamps are those where two or more stamps with different designs are joined. Sometimes it will take the entire se-tenant unit to complete a design. In other instances stamps of completely different design and face value have been printed se-tenant. Stamp collectors prefer that se-tenant stamps remain intact.

Another French term used in stamp collecting is **tete beche**, which means *head to tail*. Tete beche stamps are those were one stamp has been printed upside-down in relation to the stamp next to it. Tete beche stamps must be collected in unseparated pairs because to separate them would eliminate the tete beche feature.

## Cinderellas

Stamp collectors frequently acquire stamplike items that have no postal validity and were not used for revenue purposes. These are called cinderellas, an analogy to the fairy tale about the destitute young woman who went to a ball looking like a princess. A cinderella stamp looks like a postage stamp but does not pay for a postal service. This broad category of collectables include Christmas seals and other labels that raise money for charity, poster stamps that advertise events or products, trade stamps businesses give to customers to generate repeat business, and a host of other stamplike labels. Cinderellas are not postage stamps, but are of interest to some stamp collectors.

LEFT: A tete-beche (head to tail) pair of 20 centimes post rider stamp issued by Switzerland in 1960. RIGHT: Stamp collectors call non-postal labels such as this one "cinderellas." It was released by the U.S. Olympic Committee for the London 1948 Games.

### CHAPTER FOUR

# TOOLS FOR
# STAMP COLLECTORS

## What You Need and How to Use Them

Some hobbies and sports need a lot of expensive equipment just to get started, but stamp collecting is not one of them. While the start-up cost for beginning stamp collectors is far less than for many other activities, getting the right tools will assure a beginner of getting the right start. Most stamp tools must be acquired through stamp supply dealers, but many of them may be found at local office-supply stores.

Among the items useful for beginning stamp collectors: rotary and guillotine paper cutters that are useful for cutting stamp mounts quickly and evenly; acid-free paper for making your own album pages; glue sticks; paper testers that check paper to determine if it is acid free; high-quality page protectors; padded binders with matching slipcases that make superb stamp albums; and light boxes for making tracings of postal markings or illuminating stamps from behind to check for damage.

More sources for stamp collecting supplies are listed in Chapter Ten.

### The Essentials

The essential equipment needed by stamp collectors is surprisingly minimal and budget-friendly. As a collection grows and the collector becomes more sophisticated, other equipment may be added.

OPPOSITE: Perforation gauges.

Stamps are the one thing a stamp collector really needs to get started. Without stamps to examine and enjoy, a beginning collector will lose interest very quickly. The most likely place for a new collector to acquire stamps is from his or her own mail and from the local post office. Chapter Five has more information about acquiring stamps from other sources.

There are two other pieces of equipment that a stamp collector must have.

## Stamp tongs

The single most important piece of equipment a stamp collector can own and use is a pair of stamp tongs. Stamps are fragile. Careless handling will damage them. The best way to avoid careless handling is by using stamp tongs to pick them up and place them in mounts, on album pages, or in stock books. Using tongs reduces the risk of creasing the stamps, damaging the perforations, disturbing the gum on mint stamps, or accidentally transferring oil from hands to stamps. Picking up stamps with your fingers is not a good idea. No matter how well

you wash your hands before working with stamps, your hands and fingers will still have a protective film of natural oil that will be absorbed by the porous stamp paper. It is unlikely the result of this transfer will manifest itself immediately, but over time the oil can discolor or stain the stamp.

Stamp tongs look like eyebrow tweezers, but they don't have groves in their tips like eyebrow tweezers have. They are made of springy metal requiring only a light touch to grasp a stamp. Some tongs have rounded spade-shaped tips. Others have pointed or angled tips. They come in a variety of lengths. Try all styles of tongs to see which are the most comfortable for you to use. Look for tongs that are balanced, fit comfortably in your hand, and open and close with minimal effort.

Using a pair of stamp tongs takes practice. Stamp tongs usually have ribbing halfway down each shank where the finger and thumb will find a natural grip. Grasp the tongs between the thumb and index finger. Gently squeeze the tongs. With a little pressure, the two ends should meet perfectly. Try this a few times, and then try picking up a stamp with the tongs by sliding one of the open ends under the stamp. Use care when doing this so that you neither poke a hole in the stamp, nor bend it in any way. This may seem awkward at first but once you get into the habit of using tongs every time you pick up a stamp, it will become very natural.

## Stock book

Keeping the stamps safe and available to enjoy is a priority. Stamps are small and delicate. They can be easily lost or damaged, so it is a good idea to put them in a safe place. Placing stamps loose into a desk

Proper use of stamp tongs and a magnifying glass is shown on this 1979 stamp from Egypt.

Stock books come in a variety of colors, sizes, and formats. Stock books are excellent for storing stamps.

drawer or shoebox is not only unsafe, it also does not allow for easy viewing or enjoyment of them.

A **stock book** is an unprinted album where the stamps can be slid behind strips of glassine or archival plastic film and still enjoyed. Many sellers offer great buys on stock books in every price range, and stock books can be used later for safely storing duplicates.

Stock books will hold stamps without any additional mounting materials. Stamps are inserted into the stock book by lifting the glassine or plastic strip slightly away from the backing. Carefully use tongs to tuck the stamp behind the strip. If done properly, none of the corners of the stamps will be bent, all of the perforations will remain smooth and flat, and the stamps will not get torn.

## Nonessential Equipment

Stamps, tongs, and a stock book are the three essentials for new collectors. With these a collector can learn a lot about stamp collecting, experience all the fun of the hobby, and go a long time without having to purchase any other supplies or equipment. Eventually, as a collection grows, most collectors will want to add catalogs, a perforation gauge, magnifiers, albums, mounts, and other equipment.

### Catalogs

Stamp catalogs contain stamp illustrations, catalog numbers, values for stamps, gauges of perforations, types of watermarks, and other information about stamps. Catalogs may contain listings of a single country, a grouping of countries, a specific time period, or a particular topic. Very detailed catalogs have been published for a single stamp or set of stamps that have many different collectable varieties.

Arranging a collection in a stock book does not require a lot of collecting supplies, but adding stamp catalogs for the countries or topics you have decided to collect will help you organize, appreciate, and keep track of your collection.

Catalogs can be an expensive acquisition, but many public libraries in the United States have a set of the *Scott Standard Postage Stamp Catalogues* that are used most often in the United States. Other excellent catalogs are published throughout the world (see Sources in Chapter 10). No matter what catalog you use, take the time to read the introduction. This will explain how the catalog is organized, the terminology the catalog publisher uses, the methodology used to determine "catalog value" of individual stamps, and other pertinent information. The catalog might even have instructions on how to

Stamp catalogs contain information about how stamps are printed, perforated, and watermarked, the dates stamps were issued, the subject illustrated on the stamp and values for stamps.

use it. It takes time and lots of practice to learn how to identify and look up a stamp quickly, but cataloging is one of the most fundamental skills a stamp collector needs to develop.

Once you have read the introductory pages in the catalog, select the volume that will contain the stamps from the country or area you wish to look up. The *Scott Standard Postage Stamp Catalogue* is a worldwide catalog that currently numbers six volumes for the countries of the world, arranged alphabetically. (Many stamp catalogs today are issued in both print and CD-ROM versions.)

The stamp illustrated here is from the Cook Islands, an archipelago in the South Pacific Ocean, which is found in *Scott Standard Postage Catalogue,* volume two, containing countries of the world beginning with the letters C through F.

The first step to finding a stamp in this catalog or any other is to seek an illustration that bears some resemblance to it. The picture of the stamp will have a short description and an illustration number beneath it. Not all of the numerous stamp

designs are illustrated in catalogs. Sometimes you have to try to match other design elements such as frame styles or vignettes.

The Cook Islands stamp is shown in the catalog, described as "Landing of Capt. Cook" and with an illustration number of "A12." The illustration number is not the same as the catalog number. An illustration number might refer to several looka-like stamps, each of which will have its own unique catalog number. To find the catalog number, you have to look at all the stamps with the same design type number. Find the description that exactly matches this stamp by process of elimination.

This catalog has three different stamps listed for illustration number A12. The first is listed in a section that begins with headings that read "Unwmk." (meaning the stamps in this section are unwatermarked), "1932, Mar. 16" (meaning all of the stamps listed in the section were first released on

There are three different catalog listings for a stamp that resembles this ½-penny stamp from Cook Islands. A step-by-step process helps collectors catalog the stamp.

March 16, 1932), "Engr." (meaning all of the stamps in this section were engraved [intaglio] printed), "Perf. 13" (all of the stamps have perforations that gauge 13 on all sides unless otherwise noted), "Center in Black" (all of the stamps have a vignette in the center that is printed in black). This version of the "A12" stamp is described as "½d deep green." The catalog number for this stamp is referred to as "Cook Islands Scott 84." There is also a subvariety of this stamp listed as "Perf. 14." The subvarieties are listed below the main listing, indented slightly with a subvariety letter. In this case it would be "a. Perf 14." The *Scott Catalogue* number for the subvariety is "Cook Islands Scott 84a."

The second listing is for " ½d deep green and black" issued in 1933. This time there is a watermark, described as "Wmk. 61," illustrated at the beginning of the listings for Cook Islands. That watermark is a single star with the letters "NZ" (seen from the back of the stamps these letters would look reversed) close to and above the star. This watermarked stamp has perforations that gauge 14, and it would be referred to as "Cook Islands Scott 91."

The description for the final listing for "A12" is "½d dark olive green and black," engraved, "Perf. 14," with watermark 253. This watermark is also illustrated at the beginning of the Cook Islands listings. This watermark is described as a multiple NZ and star design. The difference between this watermark and the previous one is that it is an all-over repeating design instead of just one single watermark. This is called "Cook Islands Scott 116."

So which stamp is this? All are engraved, so the printing will not answer that question. Measuring the gauge of the perforations will help, but that would not be the fastest way to catalog this stamp because two of them are "Perf. 14" and one is "Perf. 13" but that one also has a "Perf. 14" sub-variety. However, each of the stamps has a different listing for watermarks. Scott 84 has no watermark. Scott 91 has a single NZ and star close together watermark, and Scott 116 has a multiple NZ and star watermark. The fastest way to correctly catalog this stamp is to flip it over and check the watermark (see Watermark Devices in this chapter).

This stamp has a single NZ and star watermark, making it "Cook Islands Scott 91." This stamp has a current catalog value of $1.10 mint (a stamp that has not been canceled) and $5.00 used. The catalog value should be used as a guide to pricing and not necessarily what you would have to pay for a stamp if you wished to purchase it, nor the price you could expect to receive if selling. See Chapter Eight for more information on factors that affect stamp value.

Acquiring a specialized catalog is especially helpful for collectors who limit their collecting activity to just a few countries. Specialized catalogs will often give much more detailed information about varieties, errors, shades, watermarks, and printing. Some specialized catalogs will value stamps still on envelopes, called **covers** by stamp collectors. At best these values can only be used as a rough guide. The value of an envelope with stamps is subject to many variables. They include the method of delivery, markings on the envelope, whether other stamps are also on the envelope, the destination, and of course, condition. This will be discussed to a greater degree in Chapter Six.

# Looking for Clues on Stamps

Some stamps might have clues to help you find them more quickly in a catalog. The year of issue might be printed somewhere on the stamp. The Cayman Islands stamp illustrated here has the dates at the top of the stamp "1923–1948," commemorating the Silver Anniversary of the marriage of King George VI and Queen Elizabeth. To find the stamp quickly in the catalog, you need only look for those listings for Cayman Island that appear for the year 1948. Other stamps have the year of issue printed in tiny type somewhere in the bottom margin.

Physical appearance of stamps frequently offers clues that will help a collector find them more quickly in a catalog. Stamps from the nineteenth and early twentieth centuries were usually heavily ornamented and printed in only one or two colors. More modern stamps have far less ornamentation and are printed in multiple colors.

The denomination of a stamp also aids in faster cataloging. If you are seeking a stamp from Germany that has a 12 pfennig denomination printed on the stamp, only look in the catalog for 12 pfennig stamps.

Savvy collectors will use portraits of reigning monarchs that appear on stamps of the British Commonwealth and other kingdoms to locate quickly those stamps in catalogs.

The use of catalogs creates a need for other equipment such as a perforation gauge, a watermark tray, and watermark fluid. Different gauges of perforation might mean big differences in the values of stamps, and the same is true of watermarks. Both perforations and watermarks are vital to the correct identification of a stamp and the correct placement of a stamp in a printed album.

Not all stamps will have multiple listings as did the ½ penny Cook Islands stamp. Most stamp designs will have only one listing, but some stamps are even more complicated than the one from Cook Islands. These complex stamp listings can be broken down to steps. Pay attention to differences in printing, perforations, watermarks, and any other pertinent details noted in the catalog. It takes practice and patience, but cataloging stamps is a skill you can learn.

## Stamp identifier

It is easy to figure out where a stamp came from if the country name is printed boldly in English or other languages with which you are familiar. What if the stamp has the country in a Cyrillic alphabet that you can't read, or Asian characters, or only has a symbol representing the country?

Many stamp catalogs have a section that will help identify these kinds of stamps. Several good stamp identifiers have been published (see "Sources" in Chapter Ten). Stamp identifiers are usually organized by groupings and have lots of illustrations, making it a simple matter to match the markings on your stamp with those depicted in the stamp identifier.

Finding a stamp in a catalog requires a little detective work. Clues on this stamp from Cayman Islands are dates at the top of the stamp and the reigning monarch.

A stamp identifier will aid with difficult inscriptions on stamps. Illustrations from left to right, are stamps from Bosnia Herzegovina, Japan, and Montenegro.

## Reference works

Stamp collectors are fortunate because of the massive body of reference works, specialty journals, books, and catalogs available to them, but the sheer number of publications can be overwhelming.

Many collectors make the mistake of not factoring into their annual stamp budget the purchase of a few vital catalogs and reference works. Having even a few basic books sharing shelf space with your albums will enhance appreciation of your collection and provide you with the knowledge needed to spot a good value. In any field, knowledge is power.

Your collecting interests will dictate the reference works you should acquire, but it does not matter if you collect one country or the whole world—your first acquisition should be a catalog. If you have and use a recognized general worldwide catalog, you will be able to use that numbering system to make your purchases, comparison shop,

and keep a concise inventory of your collection.

There are many good, basic books available to stamp collectors. (Recommendations on titles and sources may be found in Chapter Ten.) A stamp catalog and one or two basic reference works are the starting point for a stamp collection library. Knowing what books to buy is at least as important as knowing where to buy them. Ask the dealers with whom you do business to recommend titles to you, and never pass up the opportunity to peruse the offerings of philatelic literature dealers at stamp shows, shops, and online.

Many auction houses produce lavishly illustrated color catalogs. Some are available free upon

A variety of reference works give collectors a better understanding and appreciation of their hobby.

## The "P" Word

What is that word that starts with a P that stamp collectors use?

The word is *philately*, pronounced phil-AT-eh-lee, and it means stamp collecting. The root words are "philos" from the Greek meaning *love*, and "atelia" from the Greek meaning *tax exemption*. This refers to the postal reforms discussed earlier where a properly stamped letter was free from any additional taxes or fees for service.

Collecting and studying stamps is called philately. Stamp collectors are frequently called *philatelists* (phil-AT-eh-lists). The adjective *philatelic* (phil-ah-TELL-ick) is used when describing anything of interest to stamp collectors.

This book uses the more commonly understood "stamp collector" and "stamp collecting" whenever possible. However, there is no single good corresponding plain English adjective with the same meaning as "philatelic," and so that is used when appropriate. It means "relating to stamps or stamp collecting."

request. Others might require an initial subscription, but once you buy at an auction regularly, most firms will send you future catalogs gratis.

Auction catalogs often provide color illustrations of rarely seen stamps, and prices realized at auction are sent to bidders on request. These can provide invaluable market information. Occasionally, the auction catalog of an outstanding collection will become a landmark reference for the field.

The American Philatelic Research Library (APRL) has its card catalog available online at www.stamps.org. Searching the card catalog for a specific area of interest might turn up some interesting titles. Members of the American Philatelic Society may borrow items of interest from the APRL for a small fee, just one of many services provided to its members.

Investigate new titles published by stamp organizations and specialty societies. Many stamp collecting books are published in extremely short print runs. Books that pertain to a popular subject are quickly absorbed into the marketplace, so sometimes you need to buy right away.

Hundreds of specialist organizations serve nearly every whim a stamp collector might imagine, from U.S. stamps to topical collections of masks on stamps. Membership will usually bring a newsletter or journal devoted to the group's specialty. The journal alone is worth the price of membership, but add to that the priceless value of networking and making friends with people who share your passion.

### Perforation gauge

Perforations are the holes punched between stamps to make it easy to separate one from the other. They are measured by the number of holes per twenty millimeters (two centimeters). Die cuts are measured from peak to peak or valley to valley.

Anyone who has ever looked at the listings in a stamp catalog knows that one of the important identifying features of most stamps is the measurement of the perforations or die cuts. Stamps that look alike can have different catalog numbers and vastly different values based solely on the measurement of the perforations.

Using a gauge makes checking these measurements a simple process. It is accomplished by using tongs to slide a stamp along the guides until the teeth or peaks perfectly match the guidelines on the

Slide a stamp along the scale on a perforation gauge until the perforations exactly match the marks. The corresponding number is the gauge for that side of the stamp.

gauge. The measurement number is printed on the scale. When a stamp is aligned on the perforation gauge so that all the "teeth" (the parts of the perforation that stick out) match the guidelines or marks, this gives a measurement of the number of perforations per two centimeters. Many stamps have different perforation measurements for the tops, bottoms, and sides. When this happens, the measurements are given for the top first and then for the side.

There are many different perforation gauges from which to choose. Several manufacturers have ones that are clear. This is useful because it allows the accurate measurement of stamps that are still on envelopes. Some perforation gauges will also have a millimeter scale, a centerline ruler (useful for neatly placing stamps on a blank album page) and a gauge that measures the size of circular cancellations. Try several perforation gauges to find one that works well for you.

## Watermark devices

Watermarks are security features that deter counterfeiting of stamps and other accountable paper. Watermarks are really nothing more than a slight thinning of the paper in a pattern or design that can be viewed when the paper is held to a light source or put into a fluid specifically designed to show watermarks.

A large number of stamp watermarks can be readily seen from the back of the stamp and need no special equipment.

Some watermarks are not prominent and require an aid to see them. Many devices have been invented for this purpose, but the simplest, least expensive, and arguably the most effective is a small, black plastic or glass watermark tray. Place the stamp face down in the tray. Often this will be enough to allow the watermark to show, but in more stubborn cases, a few drops of watermark fluid might be necessary.

Watermark fluid is available under a variety of commercial names (see "Sources" in Chapter Ten). Some collectors use lighter fluid (naptha). Although this works, it can leave a harmful

Use a watermark tray and watermark fluid to view difficult-to-see watermarks.

residue and stamps treated with lighter fluid dry more slowly.

Use watermark fluid with great care. Never use watermark fluid in an enclosed area because some watermark fluids have toxic fumes. Never use it around open flames because most brands are highly flammable. Never allow children to use watermark fluid without adult supervision.

Using watermark fluid is simple. Use stamp tongs to place a stamp face down in a black plastic or glass watermark tray. Put a few drops of watermark fluid on the stamp. Allow the fluid to penetrate the stamp for a few seconds and the watermark will become visible for a brief time before the fluid evaporates. Most watermark fluid is designed to evaporate very quickly, but it is always a good idea to use stamp tongs to remove the stamp from the tray and put it on absorbent blotting paper or paper towels for a few minutes before placing the stamp in an album or stock book.

Using a tray and fluid is the most economical method of watermarking, but other equipment is also available. There is an electronic box that uses lights to make the watermarks visible. Another method uses fluid-filled plastic pouches that are placed over the stamps. The pouch is rubbed with a roller and the design of the watermark appears in the fluid-filled pouch.

## Magnifying glass

A good magnifying glass is imperative for collectors who are looking for the secret marks found on nineteenth-century United States stamps, for microprinting that appears on modern stamps, and for other kinds of stamp varieties. A magnifier also

A collector uses stamp tongs to insert a stamp into a stamp album on this 1964 stamp from Wallis & Futuna Islands in the South Pacific Ocean.

allows greater appreciation of the fine detail in stamp designs.

Magnifying glasses and scopes can be found in a variety of sizes, powers, and prices. Collectors may wish to acquire two magnifiers—one for ordinary use and a more powerful one for fine detail viewing. Try them out before making a purchase.

## Stamp albums

Many—perhaps most—stamp collectors use printed stamp albums for all or part of their collections. There are numerous advantages and some disadvantages. High on the list of advantages is that it is an easy and attractive way to safely display and enjoy the collection. An album is easy to thumb through, but care should be taken when turning the pages so that stamps do not get bent.

Printed albums require supplements to keep them updated for new stamps that are issued each year. Although stamp albums exist for some topical subjects, most stamp albums are set up for a single country, a group of related countries, or for a worldwide collection. Stock books or self-made albums are excellent choices for collecting themes or topics for which no printed albums exist.

Selecting a stamp album can be overwhelming. There are many publishers from which to choose, and every collector needs to evaluate appearance, cost, durability, functionality, ease of use, and availability of supplements to meet their needs. The most important consideration should be the safety of the stamps that will be contained within the album. All materials that will come in contact with stamps should be archival quality. Albums that have pages with illustrations printed only on one side are superior choices. (Albums whose pages are printed on both sides pose a problem because stamps hinged in

France – Semi-Postals

| | | | | |
|---|---|---|---|---|
| 1939 Postal Museum | 1940 Victims of War | 1943 Bomb Victims | 1944 Cathedrals | 1944 Cathedrals |
| 1944 Cathedrals | 1944 Stamp Day | 1944 Birth of Sarah Bernhardt | 1945 Child Welfare | 1945 Destruction of Oradour |
| 1946 Fight Against VD | 1946 Fight Against Cancer | 1946 Disabled Veterans | 1946 Postal Museum | 1946 Stamp Day |
| 1947 Cathedral | 1947 Stamp Day | 1947 Liberty Highway | 1948 Stamp Day | 1948 French Revolution |

Do-it-yourself album pages are easy to make using a home computer, blank paper, and a printer.

such albums can pull on one another and cause tears, creases, or lost stamps.)

Home computers are useful for a variety of tasks in stamp collecting. Stamp collectors use computers to search the internet for items to buy and information on the stamps they already own. Some collectors keep an inventory and make checklists of the stamps they have in their collection using their computer. You can also make simple album pages with or without text using word processing software and then print the pages with a laser or inkjet printer.

### Hinges and mounts

The use of an album poses another dilemma for a collector. A choice must be made about whether to use stamp hinges or stamp mounts.

Stamp hinges are small, inexpensive rectangular pieces of gummed glassine paper. About one-third of the hinge is folded. The short third is lightly moistened and applied to the stamp and the other portion is moistened and applied to the album. Once stamp hinges were the only good method to safely place stamps in an album. Hinges used to be manufactured so they would peel away safely from both the stamp and the album without damaging either, but they are no longer as peelable as they were several decades ago. When removed, most hinges today leave a trace of themselves on the stamps and on the album pages—or they peel away part of the stamp or album page.

The risk of damage from poorly made stamp hinges can be minimized with proper use. Today most hinges are pre-folded. This means that about a third of the hinge has been folded over, gum-side out. To hinge a stamp onto an album page, hold the stamp firmly with stamp tongs. Lightly moisten the short end of the folded hinge. Use as little moisture as possible. Too much moisture on a hinge will cause the gum to ooze off the hinge and onto the album page. The stamp will either become permanently stuck to the page, or it will not stick at all.

Affix the moistened short end of the hinge to the back of the stamp as near to the top of the stamp as possible without overlapping the perforations. Then lightly moisten the bottom third of the long end if the hinge. Do not moisten the entire back of the hinge—just the bottom third. Use tongs to apply the stamp to its proper place on the album page, and then pull the stamp up and away from the page using the tongs. This little trick virtually eliminates "stuck down" stamps and assures that the stamp works as though it is on a hinge.

Do not try to pull the stamp off right away if it is mistakenly put in the wrong place. Allow it to dry for at least a half hour and then carefully pull the stamp and hinge from the album page. Should you wish to remove a hinge from the back of a stamp, give it a gentle tug. Stop if the hinge does not come away easily from the stamp. (More drastic methods of hinge removal are covered in Chapter Seven, "Soaking and hinge removal techniques).

Stamp mounts are double strips of polyester film or other inert plastic material that are heat-sealed on one or more sides. The most common mounts are sealed at the top and bottom with a backing that is split so a stamp can be inserted. Another type is open on three sides and heat sealed on the bottom. These do not hold the stamps as securely as those sealed at top and bottom, but they are easier to fit to the size of a stamp. Both styles of mounts are gummed on the backs. When slightly moistened they can be affixed to an album page. Mounts come in long strips that must be cut to size, or can be purchased pre-cut.

If using long strips of mounts, measure the stamp top to bottom and side to side. Select a mount the proper height for the stamp. The stamp should fit the mount with a little space left over. The perforations should never be jammed against the sealed edges of the mount. Cut the strip a little large so that the stamp perforations lie within and away from the edges of the mount. Using a small paper cutter will assure straight cuts. Use tongs to insert the stamp into the cut mount. Lightly moisten the top of the gummed backing and place the mounted stamp in the proper place within the album.

Stamp mounts can be obtained with either clear or black backgrounds. The black background makes the colors of the stamp stand out, but if the mount is not cut absolutely straight the result can make the album pages look sloppy. Mounts with clear backgrounds blend into the page so it is not so critical to cut the mounts with perfectly straight edges.

Stamp mounts are expensive and they add

Stamps are held into place in stamp albums by the use of stamp hinges or stamp mounts.

considerable bulk and weight to a stamp album. They usually cannot be peeled from an album page without damaging the page, and they require acquiring a variety of sizes to accommodate a multitude of different size stamps. However, mounts do protect stamps better than hinges and a stamp can be removed from a mount and put back easily with no damage to the gum side.

Some stamp albums can be ordered with the mounts already in place for each stamp. These are great time savers, but are more expensive.

## Ultraviolet lamp

Many countries apply phosphor or fluorescent tagging to stamps. When exposed to ultraviolet light the phosphor or fluorescence triggers automatic sorting, facing, and canceling machines set to detect the tagging. Initially tagging took the form of a coating applied to the surface of the stamp, after the stamp design was printed. Today, most stamps are printed on prephosphored paper.

Phosphorescence is usually visible only with the use of an ultraviolet (UV) lamp. These come in longwave and shortwave styles and in many forms and price ranges. They may be supplied with electric current from a wall outlet or be powered by a battery.

Longwave UV is relatively harmless and can detect tagging on some foreign stamps. For detecting tagging on most U.S. stamps, you will need a shortwave UV lamp. Be careful when using a shortwave UV lamp. Prolonged indirect exposure or gazing directly into the light can burn the cornea of the eye and cause cataracts. Prescription glasses provide some protection, but using protective gog-

An ultraviolet lamp is necessary to view phosphorescent or fluorescent properties of stamps.

gles is a good idea. Shortwave UV can also cause damage to your skin. For prolonged use, it is a good idea to wear gloves and long sleeves.

Using a UV lamp is quite simple, but it needs to be done in a darkened room for optimal results. Arrange the stamps to be checked so that they do not overlap one another. Turn off any light in the room, then switch on the UV lamp and hold it so that its light strikes the stamps. If there is tagging, it will glow when exposed to the UV light.

## Color guide or key

Color guides or color keys look like paint chips or paint charts, with blocks of color that have been identified with color names. A stamp is placed next to the color chip and compared until a matching chip is found. A color guide might help a collector differentiate between a common stamp and a scarce color variety, but the best color guides are actual stamps. Unfortunately, color descriptions used by stamp catalogs are not uniform. The same shade of blue may be called "ultramarine" in one place, and "chalky blue" in another. Different catalog publishers will use different names to describe the same color.

### CHAPTER FIVE

# FINDING STAMPS FOR YOUR COLLECTION

It used to be that a stamp collector could put together a reasonable collection just from the daily mail. Today postal meters and permit impressions have largely replaced stamps, but it does not hurt to keep watching the daily mail for unexpected surprises. If family and friends save their incoming envelopes for you, your chances to find good material increase exponentially.

Buying stamps is an integral part of being a stamp collector. Every collector needs to know how to get maximum value for the money available for stamp collecting. Where and how you should buy stamps depends on the type of collection you are building and how far along you are in the process. A general worldwide collector's needs are quite different from those of a specialist. A novice collector has vastly different needs than someone who has been spending time and money on a collection for decades.

## Free Stamps from Your Daily Mail

Your daily mail is a good place to start a stamp collection. The advantages are obvious: The stamps come directly to you and they are free for the taking. There are disadvantages, too. Most of what you receive in the daily mail will be bulk mail sent only with a printed permit inscription

OPPOSITE: The daily mail is a good place to begin looking for stamps for a collection.

and no stamp. The stamped mail you get will likely have small-sized regular issue stamps affixed to it. While these are fun and interesting to collect, you will soon be swamped with them and will want more variety.

## Your Neighborhood Stamp Dealer — The Local Post Office

Every local post office is potentially a source of new stamps for stamp collectors. Postal services around the world release tens of thousands of new stamps every year and they sell most of them at local post offices.

Knowing what is likely to be on sale at any given time is not always easy. Often post offices have posters showing new stamps and the date they will go on sale. Ask postal clerks what stamps they have available for sale to collectors. This usually results in the clerk showing all of the stamps assigned to them to sell, and you might find some great surprises that way. You will have the most success by timing your visit to the local post office when it is less busy.

Larger post offices in the United States now have commemorative stamps prepackaged on cards

Your local post office has current stamps. Ask a clerk to show you new stamps.

that have been shrink-wrapped and hang on peg-boards. This makes shopping for new stamps very easy because you can see all of what is available and select the best examples at your leisure.

Postal workers sometimes characterize stamp collectors as demanding and difficult customers. Treat postal clerks with courtesy and consideration and you are much more likely to come away with the stamps you wanted.

## Buying Stamps from Postal Administrations Around the World

It is much easier to buy stamps directly from postal administrations around the world now that so many of them accept credit cards for purchases. Buying new issues directly from the source has certain advantages and disadvantages that should be considered before making new-issue purchases in this way.

The advantages differ between postal administrations, but one of the best benefits is access to the new-issue information each administration provides. Some produce first-rate philatelic magazines that are sent free to their customers.

Swiss Post, for example, publishes a big color magazine, *Focus on Stamps,* about four times a year. In addition to featuring detailed information about each new issue, there are articles on general subjects that any collector would find useful. A recent issue contained a three-page article on how holograms are produced and printed as a stamp image. The same issue contained a thematically related article on Swiss Railways. (See "Sources" in Chapter Ten.)

The United States Postal Service distributes a quarterly catalog called *USA Philatelic.* This is a catalog of items that are for sale. It gives a brief introduction

Order new stamps from postal administrations all over the world, either through their catalogs or from their websites.

of the subjects being commemorated by the stamps, color illustrations of the stamps, and prices of new issues and other products. Orders from the catalog go to the Stamp Fulfillment Services office (known as the stamp cave because it is in large underground caverns in Kansas City, Missouri) and are mailed from there. The advantage to ordering from the *USA Philatelic* is that, unlike your local post office, many older issues are still being sold from the catalog. You can get high values, odd values, and a variety of formats, all of which might be difficult or impossible to acquire at your local post office. The U.S. Postal Service also has a useful website with many features that are of interest to collectors. Access it at www.usps.com.

Australia Post offers a small color catalog, *Stamp Bulletin.* It falls somewhere between the magazine Swiss Post produces and the straightforward catalog issued by the U.S. Postal Service. *Stamp Bulletin* contains short articles about the subjects of new issues, along with color reproductions of the stamps and the souvenir items that accompany them.

So what are the disadvantages to ordering new issues directly from the postal administrations? There is a nominal fee for shipping and handling. You cannot pick through the stock for centering or other collectible differences—you get what they send you. If you want particular marginal markings or are fussy about centering, be sure to find out what the return policies are before placing your order.

Charging purchases to a credit card is the most economical way to make a purchase from a postal administration. This eliminates currency conversion or paying check-cashing fees in a different country. Be aware that many postal administrations have minimum order requirements for credit-card purchases. This might be $20 or $50, in which case you may be encouraged to spend more than you want just to make the minimum order.

Find out how much postage and handling will cost before you place your order. While $4 or $5 is fairly standard, it could be more. Read the fine print.

Fill out the order form neatly and completely according to the given instructions when purchasing new issues directly from postal administrations. Many of the order forms are processed by optical scanners. If you are sloppy when filling out your order, you might end up with the wrong stamps.

A complete list of the world's postal administrations and links to their websites may be had from the Ask Phil website operated as a service to stamp collectors by the Collectors Club of Chicago at www.askphil.org/b38a.htm.

If you want only one or two specific sets of stamps from any given postal administration, it might be more economical in the long run to order them from a new-issues dealer. (See "Sources," Chapter Ten.)

## Mail Order and Internet Stamp Dealers: What to Buy and Where to Buy It

You can acquire current stamps from your daily mail and new issues directly from the post office or worldwide postal administrations, but there is more to collecting stamps than just new issues. Remember that postage stamps have been around since 1840. Face it, you aren't going to receive a Penny Black on your incoming mail. If you wanted one to put in your stamp album, where would you find it? What about all of those other empty spaces in the album? How do you fill them up with great stamps in the most cost-effective way possible?

It is easier to find mail order and internet stamp dealers than it is to know what to buy from them. Stamp clubs and societies have their own newsletters and journals, many of which accept advertising. Read the ads to find items you would like to have for your collection. Check for dealer credentials when selecting dealers with whom to do business. The 45,000 member American Philatelic Society lists dealer-members on its website at www.stamps.org. The website listing also has contact information including links for dealer websites and e-mail, if available. Dealers who are members of a recognized stamp dealer association or an established stamp collector society are required to conduct their business according to a strict code of ethics to maintain their membership (see "Sources," Chapter Ten).

The internet has opened a whole new marketplace for stamp collectors. Stamp dealers conduct auctions, have net price sales, and offer a variety of mixtures, packets, and collections from their own websites.

What should you buy? Large mixed lots, collections, and box lots can be a great value for general collectors who are in the early, formative stages of their collecting activity. If you buy from a dealer by mail or the internet rather than in a face-to-face transaction, you need to know the meanings of the terms used to describe the stamps being sold.

### Mixtures and lots

"Mixture" is a generic term. Mixtures may be worldwide, single country lots, or lots assembled by region, such as Scandinavia or Africa. It is also possible to buy mixtures that contain only commemoratives. Read the description carefully to know what you are ordering.

Unless it is further described, assume that a mixture will include duplication (multiple copies of the same stamp) of regular issue and commemorative worldwide stamps "on paper." An **on-paper mixture** contains clippings from envelopes and packages with the stamps still attached to paper from the envelopes. You have to soak the stamps to remove the backing paper (see "Soaking and hinge removal

On-paper mixtures are a great way to get a lot of stamps at once, but these kinds of mixtures require time-intensive labor of removing the stamps from the paper backings.

techniques," Chapter Seven). Buying mixtures of on-paper stamps is one of the least expensive ways to add stamps to your collection. By sorting, soaking, and cataloging the stamps yourself, you avoid dealer markup for these services.

Mixtures are also the best place to find recent postally used commemorative stamps and a host of stamps with collectible varieties that would be difficult to acquire in any other way.

The term **mission mixture** originally meant on-paper stamps collected by churches or other charitable organizations and sold in great bulk to dealers to raise money. These mixtures usually are heavy on definitive (regular issue) stamps. Today, any on-paper mixture with heavy duplication and a preponderance of definitive stamps may be referred to as a mission mixture, regardless of the source from which it was acquired.

**Off-paper mixtures** have had the soaking step completed for you. You will receive loose stamps no longer attached to pieces of envelopes that are ready to mount in an album or stock book. You should still expect duplication.

**Bank mixtures** are getting harder to find these days. Old-fashioned bank mixtures were stamps that had been clipped from the correspondence of banks and other commercial institutions that received lots of registered or certified mail bearing high-denomination stamps. Today this kind of business mail is generally metered. A bank mixture will normally be more expensive to buy than a standard mission mixture.

Some dealers will do a preliminary sort to weed out obviously damaged stamps, and possibly better items that will be sold separately. "Unsorted" means

Off-paper mixtures are generally more expensive because the work of removing the stamps from envelopes has already been done.

that the mixture is sold just as it was received from the source. The high values, commemoratives, or other more desirable stamps have not been "cherry-picked" from the mixture. It also means that obviously damaged stamps have not been culled out.

Some dealers offer mixtures containing only commemorative stamps, or stamps from just one country. Be prepared to pay more for these types of mixtures. The more a mixture is processed before you buy it, the more it will cost you. You are paying for the dealer's time spent preparing it for sale.

**Kiloware** refers to stamps sold by weight. (A kilogram is about 2.33 pounds.) Some U.S. dealers sell kiloware by the pound or fraction thereof. Regardless of which measuring system is used, kiloware means a stamp mixture that is sold by weight. Buying smaller lots is usually a good way to sample the stock before buying an entire kilo. Soaking and sorting two-and-a-third pounds of stamps can be a daunting task, so it is best to start with a smaller lot and work your way into handling greater quantities.

## Box Lots

A box lot is just what it sounds like—a box that contains stamps. These are best inspected in person before you buy, because once you have made the purchase it is unlikely the dealer will accept its return. Most sellers will tell you the approximate weight of the box and its contents, and whether the stamps are on-paper, off-paper, or some combination of both. The seller is likely to tell you if there are any complete envelopes (covers), and whether or not the stamps in the box are limited to a few countries or the entire world. Beyond that, a box lot is a treasure hunt. You have no idea what you might find, but you are likely to have hundreds or thousands of new stamps to sort and put away.

Processing a large lot of several thousand stamps is relaxing and enjoyable, but it is also very time consuming. Imagine if you took one stamp at a time, looked it up in the catalog, then pulled out the appropriate stamp album, found the right place to mount the stamp, and then mounted it. Multiply the time it takes to do one stamp by thousands, and you can see going through a large box lot will take hundreds of hours.

The easiest way to work a box lot is to do some preliminary sorts. Estimate how much time you will have to work on the mixture in one sitting and pull out as many stamps as you believe you can sort at one time. Begin sorting that smaller grouping by country of issue.

You can buy divided boxes that help significantly with this task. These are made to separate beads, threads, and other craft projects and are available at hobby and craft shops. The boxes are shallow and have dividers that help to keep the sorted stamps

from intermingling. The sorting trays also have lids. If you are interrupted, you can put the lid on and put the whole thing away until you can work on it again. Lacking sorting boxes, most households have a variety of small plastic containers with lids. These can be used for sorting, as long as the containers are thoroughly clean and dry.

Once all of the stamps in the box lot are sorted by country, you are ready to begin the process of cataloging them, putting them into a stock book, or mounting them in an album.

Even entry-level collectors soon find that many stamps have lookalike cousins.

Stamps that have the same design might have different perforations or watermarks, or they might even be a different color or shade. When you see annotations in an album that state "similar to 1928 issue" it is a good idea to refer to a catalog as described in Chapter Four and find out precisely what stamp you have so it can be placed in the correct spot in the album.

Your sorting will almost certainly net you some stamps that you cannot readily identify. Put them into a separate pile for later investigation. In most cases, if the mystery item is a postage stamp it can be identified by country using a stamp identifier (as mentioned in Chapter Four).

You might also find stamps that are beyond the scope of a standard stamp catalog. These could include revenues, locals, charity stamps, and other seals or labels collectively known as "cinderellas," as described in Chapter Three. Since most postage stamp albums do not have spaces for these types of stamps, it is a good idea to obtain a stamp stock book and safely house the stamps there. In a short time you may find you have accumulated an interesting, albeit slightly puzzling, new collection.

Pace yourself. Sorting stamps is absorbing and there is always that treasure hunt aspect of rummaging through a bunch of stamps. You do not have to finish sorting and mounting in one sitting. Stamps will keep.

## Packets and collections

Packets and collections can offer excellent value for some collectors, but it is wise to read the descriptions to be certain what you are getting. Packets usually contain off-paper stamps. Stamps may be **mint**, **used**, **canceled-to-order** (stamps canceled by postal authorities without doing postal service that are sold to dealers at a discount from face value) or a combination of all three. Packets may be sorted by country or region, or offered as a worldwide assortment. They are sold by stamp count rather

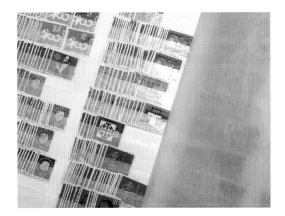

A collection generally refers to a collector-made assemblage of stamps or covers. These may be housed in albums, stock books, or some other way.

than weight, and may contain duplicated material unless specifically advertised as all different stamps.

Some dealers refer to their packets as "collections." Strictly speaking, a **collection** should be a grouping of stamps organized and formed into some sort of cohesive unit by a collector. Collections may be worldwide in nature, or organized by country or topic. They may be offered in an album, on pages, in a stock book or in glassines. A collection may contain mint stamps, used stamps, or a combination including canceled-to-order stamps.

Buying a collection in an album, on album pages, or in a stock book has several distinct advantages. Because it is already organized, you can quickly determine the extent and general condition of the collection. Use some care in this evaluation. The collector who mounted the collection may have misidentified some of the stamps. If there are expensive stamps, make sure they are what they claim to be by checking genuineness (see Chapter Eight, "Getting an expert's opinion"), perforations, and watermarks before making the purchase.

Stamps can be purchased in individual packets such as these from Ireland.

Often these collections are in very serviceable albums or stock books. You may get a nice album with a lot of life left in it that you can use for your own collection or trade or sell it to another collector. If you are thinking about beginning a single-country collection, buying another collector's specialized album is often a smart move. The fastest way to build a collection is to buy other collections.

What should you look for when buying a collection? If you are a general worldwide collector, almost anything can be of interest to you. If you specialize in only one or two countries or themes finding a collection might be more difficult, but it won't be impossible. You can find collections of different sizes, prices, and levels of completion at stamp shows, club meetings, auctions, mail order dealers, stamp shops, and on the internet.

Most of what will be offered as collections will have been made by other collectors like you who mounted stamps on pages in albums or in stock books. There will usually not be a lot of duplication, but it's always good to inspect the collection in person before you buy it, to make sure you are getting something that satisfies you. Do not expect to find valuable stamps in top grade and condition, unless you purchase a very high-end collection.

Most dealers and collectors will sell the big-ticket items separately to maximize the price they will bring. The collections from which the best material has been cherry-picked are called **remainders**. Remainder collections often still contain plenty of interesting stamps. Buying remainder collections can economically fill lots of album spaces and provide hours of stamp collecting fun.

The condition of the album and the pages upon which stamps are mounted in the remainder collection is not as important as the condition of the stamps. If you are a stickler for stamps in the very best condition, buying a remainder collection is probably not for you. Condition is likely to be mixed in collections that you will find for sale; examine the stamps you want most for your own collection closely. The overall condition of most of those stamps should be sound and without tears, thin spots made from improper removal of hinges, or visible damage. The majority of the stamps throughout the collection should lift easily from the pages. The pages and stamps should not show damage from mold, moisture, smoke, insects, or rodents.

You bought a collection chock full of stamps that was once another collector's pride and joy. Now what do you do with it? Your first inclination might be to begin immediately putting those stamps into their proper places within your own collection, but first take some extra time to look through the new acquisitions.

Remove the badly damaged stamps, but do not throw them out just yet. If they are less common varieties or forgeries, they might be useful in a reference collection. You can always discard them later after you have verified they are not useful in some way.

Check for stamps that are stuck down and take the necessary time to remove them carefully from the pages. This can be done by clipping them from the page and soaking them, as you would to remove a used stamp from an envelope clipping. (See Chapter Seven, "Soaking and hinge removal techniques.")

Watch for interesting or unusual postmarks. These can include markings of small towns, special postal services, or traveling post offices. The interesting cancels of post offices on ships, rail-roads, buses, and other types of transport might surface in a remainder collection.

Some collectors dislike perfins (perforated initials or insignia) that have been punched into stamps by businesses and governments as security devices. Other collectors love them. Whether you like them or not, some perfins are scarce and very desirable. It is worthwhile to check them in specialized catalogs.

You also might find pre-canceled stamps. Precancels, as with perfins, are loved by some collectors and loathed by others, but some of them are scarce and worth investigating. Verify watermarks and perforations, if more than one type exists. You might luck out and find a scarce variety lurking among otherwise ordinary stamps.

Once you have carefully examined the collection and removed those items that are damaged or that you have decided not to incorporate into your own collection, it is time to start mounting the stamps from the collection you purchased into your own albums.

## Approvals

Handling large quantities of stamps at one time may be too overwhelming for some collectors. If you still want to fill the spaces in a worldwide or single country collection, **approvals** may be a good choice. Stamps are sent to you, usually in sets or singles in glassine envelopes or sometimes hinged into approval books. These may be individually priced or priced as a group depending on the way a dealer does business. The advantage of buying stamps from approvals is that the arrangement

between you and a dealer is entirely automatic. Once you request approvals you will receive a package of stamps. Pick what you want, and then send the rest back with payment for the ones you kept and the process starts all over again. When you receive approvals you will have a set time limit to pay for the stamps you decide to keep and return the rest with the payment for the amount you owe. Care for approvals as you would the stamps in your own collection. If any of the approvals are damaged or lost while in your possession, you are responsible for making restitution to the dealer.

Clearly state what sort of material you want to see when you request approvals. Be as specific as possible, because the dealer will try to customize the mailings to meet your requirements. It may take some time for the dealer to begin sending exactly what you are looking to buy.

Approvals may be sold in packets like those shown here, or from approval cards or books.

| Scott # | Gibbons # | Mint | Used | Date Acquired | Vendor | Price Paid | Cat Val | Notes |
|---|---|---|---|---|---|---|---|---|
| 552 | 1046 | X | | 1994 | NZPO | FACE | 2.00 | MINI SHEET QEII |
| 553-5 | 1047-9 | X | | 1994 | | | 3.00 | |
| 556-9 | 1050-3 | X | | 1994 | G | ✓ | 3.50 | AIRCRAFT |
| 560-2 | 1058-60 | X | | 1994 | NZPO | FACE | 1.45 | CHRISTMAS |
| 563-6 | 1061-4 | | X | 1994-5 | MAIL | | 4.20 | SCENICS |
| 562-70 | 1065-8 | | | | | | 2.00 | |
| 571-6 | 1069-74 | | | | | | 4.15 | SHIPS |
| 577-80 | 1075-78 | | | | | | 4.65 | SCENICS |
| 581-3 | 1083-5 | | | | | | 1.40 | CHRISTMAS |
| 584-90 | 1086-94 | | | | | | 1.80 | ROSS DEPEN. |
| 586 | 1088a | X | | | NNIL | | .20 | PERF 14½ |
| 589a | 1091a | X | | | ( | | .20 | PERF 14½ |
| 590a | 1092a | X | | | S | | 1.40 | PERF 14½ |
| 591a | 1089a | X | | | | | 1.10 | PERF 14½ |
| 593-7 | 1110-14 | | | | | | 1.80 | |
| 598-608 | 1115-20 | | | | | | 3.15 | FARM TRANSPORT |
| 604-7 | 1121-24 | | | 1976 | NZPO | FACE | 2.80 | WATERFALLS |
| 608-10 | 1129-31 | | | | | | 1.60 | CHRISTMAS |
| 611-14 | 1085-88 | | | | | | .85 | WAR CLUBS |
| 615-9 | 1132-6 | | | | | | 1.70 | |
| 620 | 1137 | | | | | | 1.40 | QE2 MINI SHEET |
| 621-5 | 1138-42 | | | | | | 2.50 | |
| 626-7 | 1145-8 | | | | | | 1.55 | SCENICS |
| 630-31 | 1143-4 | | X | 1977 | MAIL | | .70 | PROVISIONAL SURCH. |
| 632-4 | 1153-5 | | | | | | 1.55 | CHRISTMAS |
| 635-6 | 1156-9 | | | | | | 1.35 | FIRE FIGHTING |
| 608 | 1089 | | | | | | .20 | |
| 688 | | | | | MAIL | | .80 | PERF 14/14½ |
| 644 | 1261 | | | | | | .30 | |
| 649a | | | | | MAIL | | .45 | PERF 13X12½ |
| 650 | 1185 | | | | | | 5.00 | 85 DEFIN |
| 651-8 | 1170-73 | | | | | | .80 | COILS |
| 656-9 | 1160-3 | | | 1986 | MAIL | | 1.10 | TELEPHONE |
| 660-5 | 1164-9 | | | | TRADE | | 2.20 | |
| 666-70 | 1174-8 | | | | | | 2.00 | SEA RESOURCES |
| 671-3 | 1182-4 | | | | | | 1.25 | CHRISTMAS |
| 674-80 | 1099-102 | | | | | | 2.00 | SEA SHELLS |
| 678-80 | 1185-7 | | | | | | 1.25 | STATESMEN |
| 681-84 | 1188-91 | | | | | | 1.00 | |
| 685-8 | 1192-95 | | | | | | 1.35 | SCENICS |
| 687 | 1196 | | | | | | .25 | |
| 690-2 | 1204-6 | | | | | | 1.00 | CHRISTMAS |
| 693-5 | 1201-3 | | | | | | | PROVISIONAL SURCHARGES |

A combination want list and inventory can be made using nothing more than a pencil and paper, or by using the table feature in any word processing software.

## Making purchases by using your want list

Relying on memory alone to recall the stamps you have and the stamps you need becomes increasingly difficult as your collection expands. It is a waste of resources to spend money for stamps that you already have.

The solution to this problem is to make and use a want list. A want list is an inventory of the material you seek. It contains the country name, catalog number, and an indication of whether you desire a mint example or a used one.

The most low-tech solution requires only pen, paper, a catalog, and lots of time. Keeping it simple is best. Use notebook paper and start a new page for each country. This makes it easier to update your want list and transport it to stamp shows and club meetings in a loose-leaf binder. Create a want list by going through your stamp albums, page-by-page, and writing down the catalog numbers of the stamps you need. This is time consuming, so you may wish to concentrate on one album, country, time period, or topic at a time. As you acquire stamps from your want list, cross off the numbers.

Keep receipts for any larger purchases you make. These are easy to safeguard by using top-loading page protectors that are made to fit in a ring binder. Just slip the receipts in the top-loader. Organize the top loaders in the binder, by year or month of purchase, by album, or by type or whatever makes sense for the way you collect. This will help you establish a value for the better items in your collection and will prove essential in filing an insurance claim, should the need arise.

Low-tech or high-tech, whether keeping a simple want list or a total inventory, this will become an important tool to use when ordering from a stamp dealer. Obtaining a dealer's price list is easy. All you have to do is phone, write, or send an e-mail to request one. Once you receive it, carefully read the dealer's terms of sale. When ordering by mail you do not have the opportunity to examine the stamps before making a purchase. Before you buy learn what the return policy is if the stamps you ordered are not satisfactory. Verify what catalog was used to make the price list. Catalog numbers vary between publishers.

Dealers who sell through price lists are great sources for specific items you are seeking. Gathering several price lists from different sellers is a good way to comparison shop from the comfort of your home.

## Bourses, Stamp Shows, and Stamp Shops

If you are hesitant to do business by mail, you dramatically narrow the field to dealers who sell at stamp shows, **bourses** (a venue for stamp dealers to

# Keeping Track of a Stamp Collection

Maybe you want to record more data about your stamp collection than just what you have and what you need. If so, you will want to design a database to include the type of information you will find useful. Here are a few ways to do it.

**Pen and paper**. Today most people think that a computer is required to create a database, but a database is really nothing more than a log of information. You can construct and maintain an inventory of your collection using nothing more than a pen and paper.

What sort of data might you want to log?

Perhaps you use one or more specialized catalogs whose numbers are different from Scott numbers. You could make your own concordance of catalog numbers as part of your database.

Maybe you want to track condition, grade, whether a stamp is mint or used, types of postmarks, price paid, and date and place purchased. Your database can include whatever information you desire, but the more data you have to record, the more labor-intensive managing the database becomes. As the entries become more complex it is less likely you will be able to keep up with recording the entries.

To begin, all you have to do is set up columns on a page, one column for each piece of data you want to record, such as catalog number, condition, date acquired, price paid, etc. The catalog numbers go down the page in the first column, followed in succes-

sion by the data in the remaining columns. Once you get the design of your log sheets just the way you want it, make photocopies and begin filling in the data.

**The computer**. Computerizing the data you want to track is not that difficult, and it offers advantages that a handwritten log cannot provide. Data may be sorted by date of purchase, price, catalog value, the stamps you have, or the stamps you need. You can print any number of reports, including reports that have scanned images of your stamps.

Most computers today come with software that can do the job. High-end office programs can be adapted very well to create the kinds of reports you might need for want lists, valuations, or items needing to be upgraded. Even less expensive software and freeware come with database and spreadsheet applications that will work as long as you are familiar with how to use them.

If you are not comfortable working with databases or spreadsheets, consider software made especially for stamp collectors that will get you up and running with your own personal database. The best aspect of these programs is that a great deal of the work and data entry has already been done for you, but stamp inventory software does not exist for every country or topic. Check product specifications before purchasing to verify it will work on your computer and do what you want it to do.

assemble and sell their stamps, stamped envelopes, and supplies), or who have their own shops. These are dealers that you get to meet face-to-face. You can talk to them personally, tell them exactly what you are looking for, and chat about your collection.

Purchasing sets and singles from a dealer at a bourse, stamp show, or shop has the advantage of

allowing you to examine the stamp front and back, check the condition, and make certain it is exactly what you want before you hand over the payment.

Establishing a relationship with several bourse dealers can be a real boon to your collection. Dealers will watch for special material for you and help you find it once they get to know you.

## Stamp Club Sales Circuits

Local stamp clubs and larger organizations such as the American Philatelic Society offer sales circuits to their members. Upon request, the organization will send books filled with stamps for sale from the areas you select.

Use your want list to help you choose the stamps to purchase. Fill in a transmittal slip that you return to the organization along with payment for the stamps you kept, and forward the books on to the next person on the circuit. You can also sell your own duplicates through these circuits.

A benefit of purchasing stamps from a sales circuit is that you can actually see the material you wish to purchase before you buy it because the circuits come to your own home. This allows you the opportunity of checking your collection to make sure you need the stamp you are contemplating purchasing as well as giving you time to examine the stamp. Remember that the cost of forwarding the circuit to the next collector in the circuit adds to the cost of the stamps.

## Swapping with Other Collectors

Local stamp clubs are a great place to become acquainted with other collectors. Once a relationship is established, it is fun to trade duplicates with one another. Some collectors are happy to trade stamp for stamp, others will trade using catalog value as a basis. The net result is that you get rid of your duplicates and simultaneously acquire stamps you want for your collection.

Swapping can also be done through the mail. Finding pen pals in other countries is a great way to expand a stamp collection at a low cost.

## Bidding and Buying in Stamp Auctions, Mail Bid Sales, and Internet Auctions

You will eventually want to try your luck at auction bidding. You can buy mixtures, packets, and collections at auction, in addition to individual stamps and covers.

Find advertisements for stamp auction firms in stamp publications and by searching for them on the internet. Many auction houses will send you a catalog of their next sale for free upon receiving your request. Others will charge a few dollars to send the catalog the first time. Future auction catalogs will be sent to you for free if you become a frequent bidder.

The single most important thing to do before attempting to bid in an auction is to read and understand the terms of sale. Contact the auction firm directly before bidding if you have any unresolved questions about how an auction conducts its sale.

You must know the return policy, how to pay for the lots you purchase, how they will be delivered to you if you are successful with your bids,

A huge bourse, or sales area, at the Washington 2006 World Philatelic Exhibition. An international event of this magnitude is staged in the United States every ten years.

what to do if the lots you purchased are unacceptable or not as described in the auction catalog, what your rights are if you wish to have an item authenticated, and whether or not there is a buyer's premium. Many auctions charge successful buyers a fee, usually a flat 10 or 15 percent in addition to the auction price. This information is found in the terms of sale.

The auction terms of sale contain other pertinent information you will need to know about the date the auction closes, acceptable methods of payment, how much time you will be allowed to settle your account, the amount bids will rise over next highest bids during the calling of the auction, the amount of taxes, costs you will incur for postage and insurance, and other terms that might be unique to the particular auction firm.

All of this information is very important for you to know because once you have submitted a bid you have legally agreed to abide by the terms and conditions of the sale.

Do not assume that all auction firms have the same terms of sale. They do not.

Do not rely on your memory of the terms of sale from one auction to the next because the terms might change, or you may confuse one auction with another. It takes only a few minutes to read or reread the terms and conditions of sale. Make a point of reading them before you place any bids.

Attending the auction in person is a lot of fun, but it can be dangerous if you get caught up in the heat of the action. Do your homework before you participate in any auction. Know the prices at which similar items generally sell. You should establish beforehand how much you are able and willing to

Collectors may enjoy purchasing stamps from auctions. Always read the terms of sale before placing a bid.

pay. Live bidding against others who want the same things you want can lead to overbidding. Set an upper limit of how high you will go, and then stick to it. Write those limits on the pages of the auction catalog, so you are not tempted to keep bumping up your bids. If bidding in a public auction is intimidating for you, you can hire an agent to place your bids or bid yourself by mail or phone.

Mail-bid sales are generally not true auctions and are not necessarily subject to the same terms and conditions as public auctions. It is just as important to read the terms of sale for mail-bid sales as it is for true auctions.

A big difference between mail-bid sales and public auctions is often a lack of incremental bidding in the mail sale. In these cases, the person who has placed the highest bid will often pay that price, whether it was $1 more than the second highest bidder or $100 more.

Mail bid sales can be great places to buy, but be sure you know what you are agreeing to before you sign on.

Many thousands of collectors are now participating in the online transactions offered by eBay (www.ebay.com) and other online auction sites. eBay provides a marketplace for sellers to offer their material to buyers all around the world. It uses many methods to sell, but the most common method is by auction. Generally, the seller will list a lot for a seven- or ten-day period. At the end of the period, the lot will be sold to the highest bidder at an increment above the second highest bidder. If there is only one bid, the lot is sold at the starting price established by the seller, as long as the bid met the seller's minimum.

The disadvantage of this method is that each seller establishes his own terms of sale in addition to the rules and practices followed by eBay. You will have to read every single listing to find out what the seller's policies are for returning lots that are not as described, the cost of packing and shipping, how lots that need to be expertized will be handled, methods of payment, and other pertinent information.

You might be doing business with sellers in Asia, Africa, Europe, or elsewhere. How will you get payment to them in their currency if they do not accept eBay's method to make an electronic payment? Read the policies first before you place a bid.

## More Internet Options

Sellers on eBay also have the opportunity to list lots as BUY IT NOW items. If this option is offered you can forego the auction and buy the lot immediately for the price the seller has established.

Some sellers have set up an eBay electronic store where they list net-price offerings. There is no bidding involved. If you want the item at the advertised price, you buy it, just as you would a retail item in a brick-and-mortar establishment. The various selling methods available on eBay are fully explained at www.ebay.com.

New internet auction websites are starting up all the time offering stamp collectors many additional options. Besides the auction websites, many dealers have now set up shop on the internet and have their own websites from which you can make purchases twenty-four hours a day. It has never been easier to find great stamps at competitive prices.

## Disposal of Duplicates

In buying mixtures, collections, or packets you will acquire duplicates to trade or sell that may help offset the expense of stamp purchases. What do you do with the inevitable duplicates?

Find trading partners at local stamp clubs, national or international collecting societies, or contact the dealer from whom you made the purchase. Sometimes a dealer will take unneeded items in trade for credit for future purchases. You can always create your own box lot of duplicate stamps and attempt to sell them that way.

Some clubs and societies operate sales circuits that allow their members to mount stamps on pages or booklets that circulate for sale to other members.

Stamp organizations such as the American Philatelic Society will use donated stamps in youth or adult education programs. Scouts, veterans groups, some churches, and other charities will accept donations of stamps.

Stamp donations to non-profit organizations may be tax deductible. Always verify this with your tax preparer.

# Why It Is Important to Read Auction Terms of Sale

How auction prices rise during the calling of the auction could dramatically affect the price you pay if you are the successful bidder. Most auction houses have a standard scale that escalates as the bidding goes higher.

Suppose you are willing to pay up to $300 for a particular lot. Look at the auction firm's schedule of raises and you may find that bids under $100 move up at $5 increments as bidding progresses. From $100 to $200, the bidding moves at $10 per increment. At $200, the bidding moves $20 per increment, and so on.

How does this work? If you are participating in person at the auction, you will have a card or paddle with your bidder number. You get this by registering in advance of the start of the bidding. You can also submit bids by mail, by telephone, or you can use an agent to bid for you.

The lot you want opens at $150, and there are some bidders on the floor, and some who have submitted mail bids. At $150, the bidding advances at $10 increments, so as paddles are raised, the auctioneer recognizes bids of $150, $160, $170, and so on up to $200, where the bidding goes up in $20 increments.

You continue to actively bid through all of these raises as more and more bidders fall away, until you are the only person left holding up your paddle at $220. So is $220 the price that you will pay for the lot?

No. You will pay more.

Why? Because the auction's terms of sale state that a 15 percent buyer's fee will be added to the purchase price. Fifteen percent of $220 is $33, which

will be added to the hammer price (the amount of the winning bid). You will be billed $253 plus any applicable taxes as well as postage, insurance, and packing fees if you expect your lot to be mailed to you.

If you failed to read the terms of sale before winning a lot at auction, you might be unpleasantly surprised by that buyer's fee.

In this example, the lot that you purchased contains a stamp that you know has been forged. You decide after your purchase that you should have the stamp reviewed and authenticated by experts. Before sending it to an expertizing service you had better reread both the auction's return policy and its policy for an **extension** (a hold on transfer of ownership, pending expertization).

Some auction houses will stipulate which expertizing service to use to submit purchases for expertization. If you submit to an unapproved service, then you have violated the terms of sale and the onus is on you.

Who pays the fee for expertizing? Read the auction terms of sale to find out.

What happens if the certificate from the expertizing service comes back stating that the stamp is not genuine or has been repaired, regummed, or is otherwise not as described by the auction house? You will need to know what the return policy is and how long that policy is extended if you send a stamp for expertizing. Most misunderstandings between auction firms and buyers are about lots that have been sent for expertizing, so know your rights before you bid and then follow the rules as set out by the seller.

### CHAPTER SIX

# THE ROMANCE OF THE MAILS

## What Is Postal History and Why Collect It?

Some collectors only crave stamps in mint condition, just as they came from the post office. They want stamps to have full original gum, no flaws or faults, perfect centering, and definitely no evidence of a postmark. Others like to fill their albums with stamps that have nice postmarks on the stamps showing that the stamps have done the duty for which they were issued.

Another group of collectors are more interested in **postal rates** for which the stamps were issued, the routes and methods of transport that the mail traveled and the postal markings they picked up along the way. These collectors form a branch of stamp collecting called "postal history," dedicated to the study of rates, routes, and postal markings.

Stamps were meant to be used on the mail. When a stamp is affixed to a letter that gets into the mail stream, it begins an adventure of sorts. That adventure can be unraveled by collectors willing to do the detective work. The clues can be found in the postmarks and other markings that are applied en route.

A glance at the front and back of an envelope, called a "cover" by stamp collectors, gives a collector a lot of information very quickly. With careful examination you should be able to tell where the letter originated, how much postage was paid, and where it was sent. Additional

OPPOSITE: Sorted mail.

markings add more details to the story. Some letters might have **backstamps** or **transit markings** from other post offices that help determine the route the letter traveled.

Auxiliary markings might indicate **short paid letters** for which postage is still owed (postage due). A letter with an incomplete address might have a RETURN TO SENDER marking or perhaps one that says RETURNED FOR BETTER ADDRESS. Letters sent during a war might have censorship markings. The variety is almost endless.

The postmark provides the place, date, and often, the time the envelope was mailed. A return address identifies the sender. A postmark is not necessarily the same as a cancel. A cancel is the portion of the postmark that strikes the stamps, invalidating them for future use.

## What to Look for When Collecting Postal History

An envelope can pick up all sorts of markings along the way. Here are specific examples of clues folded letters and envelopes offer to help us work out their stories.

Stampless folded letter sent from Buffalo, New York April 6, 1840 to Easton, Massachusetts. The handwritten notation "25" (cents) is the postal rate charged for delivery.

Shown here is an old stampless folded letter. There is no outer envelope. The letter sheet was folded to provide a place for the address, and sealed with a wax wafer. The letter is addressed to Easton, Massachusetts, and the blue oval postmark indicates it was mailed April 6 from Buffalo, N.Y. The letter itself reveals more information. It is a two-page letter dated April 6, 1840, to an attorney advising of the sale of a mortgage and bond and reporting on the building boom in Buffalo.

This folded letter bears no stamps because the United States did not issue postage stamps to prepay postal fees until 1847. It does bear a handwritten notation "25" in the upper right corner that indicates twenty-five cents postage. This was a lot of money in those days, but rates were calculated by a combination of distance traveled and weight of the letter. In 1840 when this letter was mailed, the postal rate in the United States for a single (one sheet of paper) letter to be carried for 400 or more miles was twenty-five cents.

During times of war, postal communications are subject to examination by military or civilian censors who determine if the letter contains information of military significance. The envelope shown nearby—sent during WWII from New Caledonia in the Pacific Ocean to the United States—is not in the best of shape, but it has been opened and examined by censors twice.

Postmarked from Noumea, August 11, 1944, the envelope was slit open and resealed on the right side by a censor, using pink sealing tape bearing a French inscription that translates as OPENED BY THE CENSOR—NEW CALEDONIA.

The numbered circular censor handstamp in

A letter mailed August 11, 1944 from New Caledonia to the United States. This wartime letter was censored by civil censors in New Caledonia and in the United States.

purple at the lower left of the envelope identifies the censor who examined the contents. A U.S. censor using cellophane "Examined by" tape resealed the left end of the envelope. This kind of tape typically turns brown and brittle over time, leaving a greasy spot behind. Nevertheless, collectors eagerly seek censored mail.

Many classifications of mail besides ordinary first-class and bulk-rate mail are familiar to us today. Express Mail, special delivery, insured mail, special handling, and certified mail are all categories of United States mail that provide extra service for additional fees.

Registered mail is one of the easiest kinds of postal history to decipher because a lot of the work has been done for you by the post office. Each letter or package that is sent by registered mail receives a unique number in the form of a label called an **etiquette** or a handstamp.

At each point along the route of delivery, the registered mail piece is recorded, and usually receives a transit marking in the form of a back-stamp. By following the dates of the backstamps, it is easy to reconstruct the route the letter traveled.

Illustrated here is a registered envelope sent to the United States from Quitandinna, Brazil on November 20,

1945. That information is garnered from the postmark that strikes the stamp and is repeated in the center of the envelope.

We know it is registered because of the hand-stamped boxed marking at the left top corner below the return address. The boxed marking is divided into thirds, with a large "R" in one block meaning REGISTERED, BRASIL, and a handwritten number in the remaining two blocks. The handwritten number is the registration number that was recorded at the post office from which this was mailed. The lower left corner has a boxed blue printed inscription that reads VIA AEREA and PAR AVION, which translates to AIR MAIL. The lozenge pattern running around the outer edges of the envelope are printed in Brazil's national colors of green, white, and yellow. This treatment is used to designate airmail and helps mail clerks sort airmail from other classes of mail.

The reverse of the envelope bears a number of backstamps that delineate the route this piece of mail traveled. The earliest readable date is an airmail marking SERVICO AERO BRAZIL dated October 21, 1945. The envelope traveled from Brazil to Miami, marked by two backstamps from Miami dated November 24, 1945. The next backstamp is a Cincinnati Registered handstamp dated November

A registered airmail letter sent from Quitandinna, Brazil on November 20, 1945 to the United States. The registration marking appears just below the hotel return address.

25, 1945 and finally a Cincinnati Oakley Station (Oakley is a suburb of Cincinnati) handstamp dated November 26, 1945.

## Soak or Save? When to Keep the Stamps on the Envelope

The used stamps found in any stamp album got there because someone removed them from the envelope (see Chapter Seven, "Soaking and hinge removal techniques"). That might not always be the best thing to do. Sometimes the stamps are better left on the envelope because the entire package—stamp, postmark, and envelope—will have an interesting story all its own.

So how do you decide whether or not it is advisable to soak? You need to do some basic sleuthing to help with decision-making.

General guidelines to consider when making the decision to remove stamps from an envelope or parcel are:

*The stamp*—Is it the right color? Are the perforations right? Answer no to either of those two questions, and you should keep the stamp on the envelope. Is it the proper denomination to pay the intended rate? Does the stamp have any noticeable error, flaw, or variety? Answer yes to these two question and the stamp should stay on the envelope.

*Postmarks and cancels*—Postmarks exist in incredible variety. They can be handstamped or applied by a machine. They can have a slogan or illustration that prints over the stamp, effectively killing it so that it may not be reused. Sometimes these slogans or illustrations can have a comical effect that would be sad to lose by removing the stamp from the envelope that contains most of the postmark. Other times a postmark might give an important clue about how the letter was carried from sender to recipient. Anything unusual about a postmark or cancel is a good reason to keep the envelope and stamps intact. Unusual postmark elements would include inverted dates; misspelled city, state, or country of posting; pictorial elements within the postmark; fancy cancels; a postmark with a significant date or place; postmarks from towns that no longer have post offices (called "D.P.O.s" or "discontinued post offices" by stamp collectors); postmarks from unusual or exotic places; manuscript signatures that had the ability to serve as payment for postage (called "free franks"), especially from famous people; ship, rail, aircraft, or postmarks from other kinds of vehicles or vessels; "First Day of Issue" postmarks; postmarks from special events such as presidential inaugurations or royal coronations.

*Famous sender or recipient*—A letter sent from or to a famous person, especially if signed or addressed by the hand of that person, is worth keeping intact.

*Auxilliary markings*—Letters can pick up an astonishing variety of additional markings to denote routings, methods of delivery, additional services, return to sender, censorship, damage in handling, and more. A good rule of thumb is to keep any envelope intact that bears an auxiliary marking. Envelopes bearing auxiliary markings such as UNCLAIMED or covers sent to a dead letter office are highly collectible. Any postal markings in addition to the postmark or cancel could be of great interest. These may include registration labels or markings; special delivery notations; backstamps or transit markings; markings indicating methods of delivery; markings explaining delays in the mail due to crashes, natural disasters, or postal complications; censorship markings; postage due notations; forwarding or return to sender instructions; and a host of other extra markings that could disclose more information about the method of delivery.

*Interesting or exotic destinations*—A letter sent from or to a country with a small population that has little mail is better left intact with the stamps, postmark, and envelope all in one piece.

*Beautiful artwork*—Many advertising envelopes contain beautiful illustrations of products that are of interest to topical stamp collectors and to those who collect advertising art. Envelopes decorated especially to receive a stamp and cancel on the first day a new stamp is issued are highly collectable and should be left together. (These are called "cachetted first day covers.")

*Eye appeal*—This quality is not easy to explain. Sometimes merely the neatness of nineteenth-century handwriting will give an envelope a lot of eye appeal, although it may not add to the value of it as a collectable. If you like the way something looks just the way it is, keep it that way and do not remove the stamp.

When in doubt, it is always best to keep the stamp on an envelope until you have more information.

## Postal Conventions, Contracts, and the Formation of the Universal Postal Union

We take it for granted today that if we address a letter and send it to a foreign country it will be delivered in due course, provided we affixed sufficient postage to pay for the service. It was not always so easy.

Prior to the mid-nineteenth century, international mails were complexities of accounting.

# Red, Blue, or Green . . . What Rate Does That Stamp Represent?

The Universal Postal Union periodically convenes congresses to discuss matters of mutual concern and to ratify new procedures. The UPU Congress of 1897 adopted an interesting practice of color coding postage stamps. The color coding was done to facilitate faster mail sorting. Stamps printed in green signified payment for international printed matter, red was intended for international postcards, and dark blue was the color for the international letter rate. It didn't matter what the denomination was or in what currency because postal clerks the world over could tell at a glance by the color of the stamp whether the proper postal rate had been paid. This color coding lasted until the mid-twentieth century, when the desire for multicolor stamps and the ability to do mechanized sorts ended the archaic UPU color plan.

Great Britain stamps from 1936 show the Universal Postal Union colors for types of international mail: green for international printed matter, red for international postal cards, and dark blue for international letter mail.

Treaties, contracts, and conventions governed the exchange of mail between countries. Postal rates varied between nations and were also dependent upon routes that were used to convey the mail. Most developed nations were participants in ten or more postal agreements with other countries. As the mail volume increased, collecting and disbursing the postal fees became arduous and exceedingly inefficient. Those who collect international mail from this time period are challenged to discover which postal agreement is applicable, what currencies may have been used to pay the postal rates, and how the letter was transported from sender to recipient across one or more international borders.

The General Postal Union was formed in 1874 to establish and maintain efficient and cost-effective exchange of mail between nations. It was renamed Universal Postal Union (UPU) in 1878 and became an agency of the United Nations in 1948. Today there are 191 nations within the UPU and its mission has expanded. The UPU not only facilitates cooperation between postal administrations around the world, but provides to them technical training and assistance.

## Postmarks and Cancels

Post offices mark postage stamps on letters and parcels with cancellations, defacing them so that they cannot be used to pay for postal services again. Strictly speaking, the word *cancel* refers only to the marking that strikes the stamp, defacing it and invalidating it for further postal use.

Cancels come in abundant variety, from simple strokes of a pen to elaborate fancy cancels that can take the form of flora, fauna, and myriad other

Machines to postmark mail, such as this one with a waving flag, began to be developed by a variety of manufacturers and used by the U.S. Post Office Department in the 1870s.

shapes and designs. Canceling devices have been carved from cork, crafted from rubber, or manufactured from steel or some other metal.

In the broadest sense of the term, a postmark is an informational marking applied to a letter or parcel by a post office. Postmarks establish the place, date, and often the time of mailing. They provide postal historians clues needed to unravel how letters traveled from sender to recipient. A clear strike of a scarce postmark can add value—sometimes significant value—to a stamp.

Postmarks existed before the invention of adhesive postage stamps. Unfortunately for collectors, many early postmarks do not have the year as part of the date. Postal history buffs are often required to do a little detective work to determine when a letter was mailed. In many cases, the year will be written on the letter within. In other cases, consultation of a specialized reference work will help narrow the possibilities.

The world's postal services have always looked for ways to increase efficiency. In the 1870s, the invention of canceling machines that automatically fed letters from a hopper and applied the postmark greatly increased the speed of postmarking. A number of different companies manufactured canceling machines, both in the United States and elsewhere. The look of the cancels differed from manufacturer to manufacturer.

Today, the mechanization process continues with an increasing number of countries using sprayed-on inkjet postmarks. The machines that apply these cancels can be programmed to apply whatever slogan is desired. New material can be acquired directly from your daily mail or from businesses that let you see their discarded envelopes.

Another popular postmark collecting field is that of commemorative and special postmarks. Commemorative postmarks are created for special events (such as the Olympics) or other special purposes. These cancels make welcome additions to topical and thematic collections. One commemorative postmark might form the hub of an entire thematic collection. Virtually all topics can be pursued with pictorial or commemorative postmarks.

## Censorship of the Mails

Postal, government, or military authorities often open and read mail during times of war or civil strife. If letters are found to contain information of a sensitive nature, that information is deleted from the missive or returned to the writer. Mail that has passed through a censor is usually marked, resealed, and sent onward to the recipient.

Censoring mail is time-consuming. The process causes many delays in the mail that hurt morale of the troops. During World War I, Great Britain developed honor pledge envelopes that were self-censored. The sender signed a pledge saying the letter contained "nothing but private and family

An honor pledge envelope, sent from British Field Post Office 886 in March 1945. It was signed by the soldier who mailed it so that the letter could bypass the military censor, but it was censored anyway.

material." (Letters in honor pledge envelopes might still be censored by military or civil censors somewhere in the mail stream.) The Field Service postcard was another method utilized to bypass a delay caused by censorship. The message side contained a set of standard messages that the sender could check. This was an impersonal way to send a message, but it did avoid the delay created by censorship and got

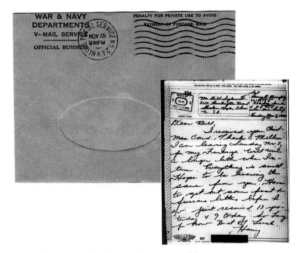

V-Mail was a method to get letters to and from servicemen serving overseas during World War II using microfilm. Rolls of microfilmed letters were sent overseas where they would be processed and forwarded to the recipient.

LEFT: An airmail letter sent from APO 922 (U.S. Army Post Office 922 in Townsville, Australia) to the United States in June 1942. Inscribed OFFICER'S MAIL, but was censored anyway. RIGHT: Airmail letter to the United States postmarked October 1941 from Colombo, Ceylon where it was censored.

that most important "I am fine" message to a worried family at home.

Some military mail was microfilmed in order to save valuable cargo space on planes and ships. A roll of microfilm could contain up to 20,000 letters. Upon receipt at the receiving station the rolls of microfilm were photographically reproduced and mailed to the addressee. Called V-Mail in the United States, it was also inspected by censors.

Military mail was usually censored by officers who would review the letters and then mark them with a handstamp, but military censors used many different types of devices to indicate that a letter had been censored. These vary widely depending upon location, branch of service, date of use, and country of origin—offering nearly endless possibilities for forming an interesting collection.

Civilian mail that was opened and examined by postal censors was resealed using either gummed paper or cellophane strips or seals. Often the censor would be required to mark the mail with an identifying number so officials could track the effectiveness of each censor without revealing his or her identity. Some censors blackened passages from letters that contained sensitive information. Others cut out and discarded the parts of the letter that did not pass the censorship guidelines. Letters that disclosed

too much sensitive information were returned to the writer.

## Unusual Methods of Mail Delivery

### United States Pony Express

The Pony Express began in April 1860. Its purpose was to reduce the time it took for mail communications across the country to San Francisco, which, until the Pony Express, took a month by sea via Panama.

The Pony Express, operated by the Central Overland California and Pike's Peak Express Company, conveyed mail between St. Joseph, Missouri, and Sacramento, California. Young men on fast horses carried letters in mail pouches, stopping to change horses at stations established along a 2,000

Arguably the world's most famous mail delivery method harkens back to America's Wild West where Pony Express riders would carry mail in saddlebags as they raced on horseback from station to station. *From the Smithsonian National Postal Museum collection.*

mile route. It was incredibly dangerous for the riders. Their journey continuously placed them in harm's way. The riders had to overcome adverse weather conditions, potentially hostile Indians, treacherous terrain, and wild animals. While an estimated 35,000 letters were carried, the Pony Express service that has become synonymous with the American "Wild West" was financially unsuccessful and ended after just 18 months, in October 1861. Letters carried by the Pony Express are rare, expensive, and eagerly sought by collectors when one comes on the market.

## Pneumatic Mail

Long before faxes and e-mail, businesses had already addressed the problem of rapid transmission of messages over long distances. Use of the telegraph was popular, but the transmitted message still had to be transcribed on paper and delivered by hand—and original documents could not be sent by telegraph. In response to this need governments of large cities all over Europe adopted a system of transmitting printed messages in pneumatically propelled capsules through subterranean tubes to their intended recipient.

Although the actual construction of the pneumatic system varied from place to place, the general

# Sending Mail Across Battle Zones

Mail could be exchanged between belligerent nations through the use of private messaging systems, the International Red Cross, and secret drop boxes. Shown here is a letter sent from Britain to Switzerland. The recipient was Helena Lubke, a Polish woman living in Lausanne. On her own initiative and with her own money, she provided trans-mailing services to Poles in occupied and Allied countries who were interred in prisoner of war and refugee camps. The envelope illustrated bears many censorship markings from belligerents on both sides of the war.

The British postmark was obliterated so that the place of mailing could not be identified. The town registration label was defaced and replaced with a London label. A German censorship strip was applied over the British label, and several other German censor markings were added.

A letter that went across enemy lines to Helena Lubke in Switzerland. The British postmark was blackened to hide the origin, and the letter was opened, examined, and resealed by both British and German censors.

Canisters filled with letters were sent from station to station using compressed air in some large cities in Europe and the United States. This was called pneumatic mail. *From the Smithsonian National Postal Museum collection.*

This envelope, sent by pneumatic tube mail, has a Chicago North Western Tube Station transit marking. *From the Smithsonian National Postal Museum collection.*

working principle remained the same: a cartridge containing small packages or telegrams would be loaded into an airtight tube. Compressed air propelled the cartridge to the end of the tube, alternatively, it would be propelled by means of suction that created a partial vacuum in the tube, depending on its destination. Mail carried in pneumatic tubes traveled at speeds as fast as 35 miles per hour.

## Tonga's Tin Can Mail

A tiny volcanic island named Niuafo'ou lies in the northern part of the Tonga group in the South Pacific Ocean. The island's iron-rich soil and tropical climate combine to produce some of the finest coconuts in the world. The coconut crop attracted commercial interest and provided income for the 1,200 Tongans living there.

Niuafo'ou lacks a safe harbor for ships or boats. Fierce ocean swells make landing supplies, including mail, very hazardous. In the late 1800s a European trader working in Niuafo'ou established a method to get mail on and off the island. Letters were wrapped in oilcloth that was sealed with wax. These packages were tied to sticks and given to Tongans

who would swim the mail out to passing vessels. When the mail volume increased, letters were placed in kerosene or cracker cans and towed to ships by swimmers. This lasted until 1931 when a shark attacked and killed one of the swimmers. Thereafter an outrigger canoe was used to transport the mail between island and ship.

In the late-1920s a German trader named Walter George Quensell began applying a myriad of handstamps to incoming and outgoing letters. The handstamps were variations on a theme that meant "Tin Can Mail." Niuafo'ou's Tin Can Mail became a popular tourist attraction for passenger cruise liners until the beginning of World War II. The envelopes the tourists sent with the exotic stamps and markings were—and still are—coveted by stamp collectors.

Envelope mailed from the island of Niuafo'ou. It was placed in a tin container, sealed and carried by canoeists to the ocean steamer *Maunganui* for forward delivery.

## Other ways the mails move

Nearly every imaginable type of vehicle has been used to transport mail from one place to another. Riders on horseback, sailing ships, bicycles, and horse-drawn coaches gave way to trains, steamboats, and motorcars. Three-wheeled motorized vehicles called

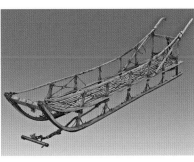

"mailsters" were used by mail carriers throughout the United States in the 1960s. Camels, elephants, pigeons, mules, oxen, and llamas have carried mail. Sleds pulled by dogs transported mail in some areas of the northern U.S. and the Alaskan Territory during winter months, and vehicles were equipped with snow skis in other parts of the country. Airplanes began carrying mail in 1911, and in 1928 an airplane carrying mail was catapulted from the deck of a French ocean liner. Enormous dirigibles carried transoceanic mails. Rockets, passenger buses, hydrofoils, autogiros, helicopters, motorcycles, and hot air balloons have all carried mail. Collectable letters transported by these many methods used for mail delivery are a testament to the ingenuity of postal services throughout the world.

## Crash, Wreck, and Disaster Mail

A **crash cover** is an envelope that survived an airline, airship, rail, or motor vehicle crash. Mail salvaged from crash sites may exhibit evidence of smoke, fire, or water damage. Salvageable crash mail is usually marked prior to forwarding it to the recipient. Shipwrecks also result in salvaged mail, and other forms of disaster may result in letters being recovered, restored, and forwarded. Mail has been rescued from fires, floods, earthquakes, storms, volcanic eruptions, riots, and acts of war.

Shown here is a postcard salvaged from the crash of the German zeppelin *Hindenburg* on May 6, 1937. The zeppelin burst into flames while attempting to dock at Lakehurst, New Jersey. The U.S. Post Office Department was able to salvage fewer than 200 pieces of burnt mail from the famous crash. Each salvaged piece was sealed in a glassine envelope before being forwarded.

The German zeppelin *Hindenburg* burst into flames while docking at Lakehurst, New Jersey on May 6, 1937. This letter was salvaged from the crash. *From the Smithsonian National Postal Museum collection.*

## First Day of Issue, Patriotic, Event, and Other Forms of Illustrated Mail

Illustrations or decorations have been added to envelopes to make them more attractive, to sell products, or to promote causes. Stamp collectors call these illustrations **cachets**, pronounced ka-SHAYS.

### First day covers

Illustrated mail is a broad collecting category that is dominated by cacheted "first day covers," or "FDCs." These are envelopes bearing a stamp postmarked on the day it was first issued, as well as some sort of an illustration that relates to the stamp subject.

First day cover collecting is a surprisingly technical and multifaceted collecting specialty. Some FDC collectors specialize in a particular cachetmaker, stamp, time period, or country. Others might collect by topic or theme. Nearly all who collect FDCs do so because these illustrated envelopes represent the birth of a new stamp, and they are intrinsically beautiful.

Besides cacheted covers, some collectors of FDCs also collect post office announcements, preliminary artwork and envelopes that bear autographs of people related to the subject of the new stamp. First-day ceremony programs are distributed to those who attend the festivities conducted by a postal administration for the release of a new stamp. These, too, are highly collectible.

### Patriotics

During times of war or civil strife, many people showed support for their country or cause by using stationery illustrated with patriotic themes. "Patriotics" can be collected by time period, conflict, subject matter, cachet designer or printer. Popular subjects for patriotic covers during times of war are flags, military heroes, maps and cartoons that depict the enemy in an unfavorable light.

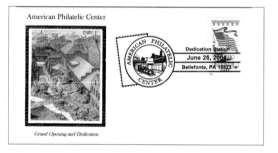

An silk cachet event cover created in 2004 for the grand opening of the American Philatelic Center, home of the American Philatelic Society, in Bellefonte, Pennsylvania.

### Events

Event covers are illustrated envelopes designed to mark a particular event. The envelope has a stamp affixed and there will usually be a complementary cancel. Illustrated event covers may include exhibitions; airport dedications; bridge openings; anniversaries of people, places, or historic events; festivals and fairs; and a host of other happenings ranging from the notable to the obscure.

Cacheted First Day Covers, or "FDCs," have an illustrated design or text that pertains to the stamp or stamps affixed to the envelope. The stamps are postmarked on the first day they were issued.

# World War II Patriotism Through the Eyes of a Japanese-American

Envelopes with patriotic cachets were produced during WWII by Etsuo Sayama. Sayama was a Nisei, a Japanese-American born and raised in Honolulu, in what was then the Territory of Hawaii. Sayama was employed as a civilian draftsman with the U.S. Army when the Japanese attacked Pearl Harbor on December 7, 1941.

Sayama's cachets bring an interesting perspective to patriotic cover collecting. They reflect Hawaiian culture as well as show patriotism from the point of view of a Japanese-American. A poignant multicolor design Sayama produced in 1944 to commemorate the third anniversary of the attack on Pearl Harbor is shown nearby. Titled "Sunset and Shadows," the cachet shows the Grim Reaper overtaking the Empire of Japan against the background of the Rising Sun of the Japanese naval ensign.

This envelope has a military free franking (military personnel did not have to pay postage on first class letters) and was mailed from Army Post Office 309 at Schofield Barracks, Hawaii. The letter was self-censored by the officer who mailed it.

A patriotic cover from 1944 shows Grim Reaper's shadow over Japan. It was created by Japanese-American Etsuo Sayama on the third anniversary of Pearl Harbor attack.

## Advertising

First day and event covers are the best-known branches of the illustrated mail field, but others are equally intriguing. Businesses have long realized that an eye-catching illustration on an envelope will compel the recipient to open and investigate the contents. Even today, colorful advertising appears on envelopes that pepper our daily mail. These can be useful additions to topical collections.

Shown here is an advertising envelope from the National Phonograph Co., mailed from New York City in 1902. This example of an advertising cover beautifully exemplifies the period from which it emanated. The cachet shows a newfangled (for its time) phonograph with its huge hornlike amplifier. The illustration itself is in the distinctive arts and crafts style that was trendy at the time.

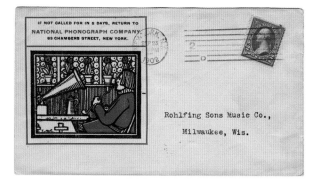

An advertising cover sent in 1908 from New York City to Milwaukee from the National Phonograph Company. Artwork was in the Arts and Crafts style that was popular at the time.

### Hand drawn, hand painted

Many people like to express their personalities by creating their own letterheads, envelopes, and notecards. Hand-drawn and painted stationery can be very appealing. Some designs are quite elaborate, such as this cover sent from Australia during World War II. The blue bird is hand-drawn and hand-painted with great skill and care. The pretty bird is a form of folk art. It is almost a pity that two censorship handstamps and resealing tape partially

A 1944 handpainted bluebird cachet, sent from Australia to the United states. It was opened, examined, and resealed by both military and civilian censors.

obscure the design, but these are reminders of the time that this unique item was posted.

### History Reflected in Daily Mail

Extraordinary current events are often reflected in the mail of ordinary citizens. An event of importance might be mentioned in a letter, which in turn gives insight to the impact that event had on the sender. This is where social history and postal history meet.

This handstamp used by postal workers was collected from the ground floor of the post office that served the World Trade Center. Last used on September 11, 2001. *From the Smithsonian National Postal Museum collection.*

Few will forget the events of September 11, 2001. The attacks on the World Trade Center and the Pentagon involving hijacked commercial aircraft resulted in drastic changes for both air passengers and cargo. Thereafter parcels carried on aircraft were subjected to more stringent regulations and screenings for explosives. A United States Priority Mail envelope postmarked February 17, 2004 bears two strikes of a handstamp that shows a plane within a crossed circle and the text SURFACE TRANSIT ONLY DUE TO HEIGHTENED AIRLINE SECURITY. A similar message is shown on an airmail parcel

LEFT: Mail container salvaged from United Air Lines Flight 93 that crashed in central Pennsylvania on September 11, 2001 to prevent hijackers from making a second attack on Washington, D.C. RIGHT: This street collection mailbox located in front of Church Street Station Post Office across the street from World Trade Center Building 5 suffered minimal damage from the attack on September 11, 2001. *Both photos from the Smithsonian National Postal Museum collection.*

sent February 9, 2004, from Canberra, Australia. The self-adhesive Australia Post label reads, Delayed for compliance with Aviation Security Regulations.

Modern postal history happens every day. It is an important record that reflects social history and serves to document the way events shape the lives of ordinary people. Today's current events are tomorrow's history.

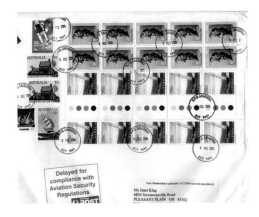

Airmail parcel sent from Australia to the United States in February 2004 with label that states Delayed for compliance with Aviation Security Regulations.

# Terrorism Through the Mail

In years past, it was believed that diseases such as yellow fever, cholera, and bubonic plague could be transmitted in the mail. During epidemics, postal services treated mail by perforating the envelopes with holes or by clipping their corners so sulfur dioxide or formaldehyde vapors could be blown into them. It was later proved that these diseases were not spread through the post, but shortly after the September 11 attacks, spores of a deadly disease called anthrax were intentionally placed in letters addressed to government and media offices. The accompanying handwritten letters seemed to connect the anthrax to the September 11 attacks, but to date the origin is an unsolved mystery.

Nevertheless, anthrax letters were responsible for five deaths and seventeen other victims who became seriously ill. The Brentwood (Washington, D.C.) and Trenton, New Jersey, mail-processing facilities required decontamination and renovation. Employees' health had to be monitored, and the safety of the mails had to be restored. Three anthrax-contaminated letters were traced to the Trenton facility in Hamilton Township, New Jersey. This facility was closed for decontamination on October 18, 2001. Contaminated mail from the facility was transported to an irradiation center in Bridgeport, New Jersey, eighty miles to the south.

Contaminated mail was zapped with radiation to kill the anthrax spores. Unfortunately, irradiation damaged some of the mail's contents. Once the irradiation process was complete, each piece of mail was sealed in what is known as an "ambulance bag" or "body bag" containing an explanation about the radiation. The Hamilton Township postal facility finally reopened March 14, 2005.

### CHAPTER SEVEN

# CARING FOR YOUR COLLECTION

## What Can Go Wrong and How to Avoid It

Stamps, stampless folded letters, envelopes, and other philatelic materials are pieces of paper. They are fragile and subject to the ravages of time. Paper can become brittle, colors can fade, and a host of other problems may develop if neglected. Fortunately, most of the calamities that befall stamp collections can be avoided by taking preemptive action. Knowing how to recognize little problems before they become big ones is paramount to maintaining a stamp collection.

### Spotting the First Signs of Trouble

"Don't go looking for trouble" is terrible advice for stamp collectors. It is good practice to "go looking for trouble" in your stamp collection once or twice a year—and more often if you suspect trouble is brewing. Take the albums out and turn each page. Look at the pages themselves as well as the stamps mounted on the pages. If you see any of the following signs of trouble, take action immediately.

OPPOSITE: Detail of 1989 souvenier sheet from Finland.

## Mildew and mold: Gray, black or rust-colored spots or discoloration

**Problem:** Mildew and mold appear on improperly stored paper. It manifests itself as black, brownish, or gray spots on the paper. Paper from the nineteenth century or earlier is subject to a special kind of mold that resembles rust stains. This is called "foxing."

**Remedy:** Remove albums and other philatelic materials from humid or hot storage areas. Non-porous surfaces exhibiting mold, such as plastic-coated binders, can be wiped with diluted chlorine bleach and left to air dry. Follow up with another wipe with a mild detergent and clear water. The bleach will get rid of the mildew and the follow-up cleaning will remove the bleach.

Stamps on mildewed or moldy album pages should be removed from the pages and allowed to air dry. Place the stamps in "quarantine" in a stock book away from other albums. Check this frequently to see if any of the stamps develop mildew.

Mold damage on paper. *From the Smithsonian National Postal Museum conservation study collection.*

Album pages that have mold or mildew might be salvaged by allowing them to air dry in a sunny location. Note that this form of treatment is likely to discolor the pages. Some collectors will treat stamps in the same manner, but this will often cause fading or discoloration of the printed surface of the stamps. Mold or mildew damage on valuable stamps should be handled by a professional paper conservator.

**Prevention:** Mold and mildew can ruin a stamp collection faster than almost anything else except fire. Humidity is the cause of most of these problems. Stamp albums and accumulations that are kept in a wet-prone basement may be attacked quickly by mold or mildew. Once that happens it is very difficult to undo. Integrating these stamps into your collection could spread the problem.

Stamps kept in very humid conditions may develop other problems. Mint stamps may become stuck to the albums, in which they are housed, or to each other. Stamps should be removed from the wet albums and allowed to dry before remounting in new albums. (Soaking techniques are found later in this chapter.)

Attics are just as bad as damp basements. They are too hot and dry in the summertime and too

The telltale rusty spots of "foxing" are exhibited on this block of six stamps from Paraguay. *From the Smithsonian National Postal Museum conservation study collection.*

cold and wet in the winter. These wide climate fluctuations are bad for anything stored there, but especially paper. Dryness can be just as damaging to stamps as moisture. In very dry conditions, stamps can become discolored and brittle. To minimize these risks, keep all of your stamps and philatelic items in the main living areas of your residence in an environment that is comfortable for a human.

### Insects: Uneven holes in paper, black specks

**Problem:** Silverfish, termites, some types of beetles, and beetle larvae and moths will eagerly devour stamp albums and stamps and then move on to books, papers, photographs, and other cherished household items if given the opportunity. The resultant damage manifests itself as holes in the paper that has been eaten and specks of black dirt left by the insects. There may also be eggs within the bindings or pages of albums to propagate future generations of stamp-eating insects.

**Remedy:** Eliminate the insects and then install sticky pest monitoring traps to avoid future problems. Remove or repair the damaged pages and stamps. Use a soft, clean artist's brush to remove the specks and check frequently for additional signs of infestation.

**Prevention:** Insects have voracious appetites for stamp collections. Your stamp collection might look like a seven-course meal to silverfish, termites,

Insect damage. Beetles, roaches, termites, silverfish, and other insects can eat stamps. *From the Smithsonian National Postal Museum conservation study collection.*

and other insects. Keep the collection on bookshelves in an area that has proper ventilation and climate control to minimize these risks. Check for insect damage often. Silverfish, roach, and beetle pest monitoring traps are commercially available and may be satisfactory at the first signs of infestation. If insects are a big problem get an exterminator in as quickly as possible.

### Rodents: Gnawed edges of albums, pages, or stamps

**Problem:** Rodents include mice, rats, squirrels, chipmunks, and household pets such as hamsters or gerbils. They will eat anything and can do a lot of damage very quickly. Their gnaw marks are unmistakable on paper and leather or vinyl albums.

**Remedy and Prevention:** Eliminate the rodents. Keep pets in their cages. Repair or replace damaged albums or pages. Philatelic materials of value should be restored by professional conservators.

## Other Common Problems to Avoid

Proper storage and common sense can help eliminate potential problems. Store your albums vertically rather than horizontally. Stamp albums should never be stacked one on top of another or stored flat. The weight of the albums will bond the stamps to the album pages.

Never use stamp albums as scrapbooks or filing cabinets unless placed in clear polyester film

pouches to isolate them from philatelic material. Some collectors clip interesting articles from stamp newspapers and put them in their stamp albums. Over time, the acid from the newsprint leeches onto the stamps and album page, darkening them and making them brittle. It is not a good practice to put anything loose in a stamp album. Loose items will move when pages are turned and could easily crease a stamp or cause it to pop off the page and become lost.

### Bends, creases, tears

Bends, creases, and damaged perforations can occur when stock books are crammed beyond capacity. A good rule of thumb for storing stamps in stock books is never overlap or stack stamps on top of one another. If strip mounts will be used to mount stamps in albums, always make certain there is a little breathing room at the top and bottom. Perforations should not be flush against the sealed edges, or they could become bent.

Even stamps that are neatly hinged into a stamp album can become bent through careless page turning, especially if the album pages are printed on both sides with stamps mounted facing one another on opposite pages. Sooner or later one will get hung up on another. The stamps will bend each other when the album is closed.

The safest way to avoid that problem is to use only album pages that are printed on one side. The second-best option is to place interleaving between facing pages. Clear polyester film—such as Melinex or buffer tissue—is a better choice than glassine. It is more expensive, but it is archival quality, will not discolor over time, nor will it damage the stamps it touches.

Stamps will become bent when they are over-stuffed in glassine envelopes. This is avoidable by using the right-size glassine envelope or by putting fewer stamps in more envelopes. A lightly bent stamp can be flattened by inserting it in a clear polyester sleeve and then putting a weighted object, such as a heavy book, on top until it lies flat. A stamp that has been deeply creased can be treated using this method, but the paper fibers have been broken and evidence of the crease will remain.

Stamps may become torn through carelessness and mishandling. Stamps should never be removed from an envelope by attempting to peel them off. Never attempt to remove a stamp hinge from a stamp while it is still wet. (Proper stamp removal techniques are discussed later in this chapter.)

Stamps that are torn, missing paper, or badly creased are often called "seconds," and their value is frequently lost. (See Chapter Eight, "Factors that affect value.")

Glassine envelopes stuffed too full will result in damaged perforations and bent stamps.

## Stains, water or liquid damage, grease

Stains can easily be avoided by never touching stamps with anything other than stamp tongs. Your hands, no matter how often you wash them, contain natural oils that will transfer to the stamps you handle and eventually discolor them.

Do not use glue to affix stamps to album pages. Glue will discolor and the stamps will be difficult to remove from the album without doing damage to both. Cellophane tape should not be used on stamps, folded letters, or covers. The tape's adhesive will ultimately discolor, turn greasy, and then fail completely—leaving behind a messy and impossible stain.

Never write on your stamps or covers with pen or pencil. Some collectors write catalog numbers on the backs of stamps, but catalog numbers may change. Many stamps have been creased or thinned by the simple act of trying to erase pencil notations from their backs. Remove notations only with a white vinyl eraser.

Do not use metal paper clips or staples within your collection. The metal will rust and leave a stain behind. Paper clips crease the paper to which they have been affixed, and staples make holes in the paper.

Food and drink stains should never be a problem because smart collectors never eat or drink while working on a stamp collection. Coffee, tea, cola, and alcoholic beverages will leave stains if spilled on stamps or stamp albums. Imagine the damage grease from a hamburger could make if dropped on an album page! Furthermore, even minute food crumbs will attract vermin, compounding the problems.

Some collectors have been known to use a dilute

ABOVE: Cellophane censorship resealing tape used by the United States during World War II left a stain on this cover from Mexico. LEFT: Glue left a stain on this stamp from Canal Zone. *Both images from the Smithsonian National Postal Museum conservation study collection.*

bleach or hydrogen peroxide solution to remove or minimize a stain from a stamp. This is not recommended because it could alter the colors or compromise the integrity of the paper. A professional paper conservator should be consulted before attempting to remove stains from any valuable stamp or cover. "Do-it-yourself" projects can go awry and cause more damage than previously existed. Some stamps are printed with **fugitive ink** that will fade, change color, or disappear completely when exposed to anything that could potentially be used to remove a cancel, including ordinary tap water.

Lightly soiled envelopes or folded letters can be safely cleaned using a dry cleaning pad. Dry cleaning

A metal paper clip rusted over time and left a stain on this cover. *From the Smithsonian National Postal Museum conservation study collection.*

pads are available at art, drafting, and archival supply stores. The pads are loosely woven cloth bags filled with powdered eraserlike particles. Squeeze the dry cleaning pad to release some of the powdery substance over the soiled envelope. Lightly rub the cloth pad over the envelope or folded letter and then used a soft, clean artist's brush to remove the soiled particles. Soft art vinyl erasers may also be used for removing pencil marks and doing light cleaning using light pressure in a circular motion.

## Sunlight, fading

Fading is also an avoidable problem. Keep albums, stamps, and other philatelic materials out of sunlight. Even artificial light may cause photochemical color changes in stamps, but sunlight's ultraviolet rays are particularly detrimental. Keep stamps in albums or archival boxes and for more protection, put those albums or boxes in slipcases. (See Chapter Ten, "Sources.") Keep the albums away from strong light sources. Never leave an open album on a desk or table that sits in front of a sunny window. The stamps will soon curl, fade, and change color.

Discoloration on covers or stamps may be caused by exposure to light or chemicals. *From the Smithsonian National Postal Museum conservation study collection.*

## Smoke and fire

Cigarette, cigar, and pipe smoke will discolor stamps. Stamps, being very porous, will pick up the odor of smoke. You may find a collection or box of stamps purchased at auction reeks strongly of tobacco smoke. Once that smoky smell permeates the paper, it is very difficult to remove. Minimize that problem by putting the stamps individually in a sealed container with dry baking soda on the bottom and the material elevated slightly over it. Limit the direct contact between them for a few days. This is time consuming and does not work on really bad cases.

A related problem with smoking around stamps is that it creates an unnecessary fire hazard. Stray hot ashes from cigarettes or sparks from lighters can set stamps ablaze. A lifetime of careful collecting can be gone in a flash.

## Thieves

Unfortunately we live in a world where we have to be concerned about theft. Stamp collections can be an attractive target for thieves because they are easily portable and can be difficult to identify. Keep the entrances to your home (or office, if that is where your collection is stored) locked at all times. Put very valuable stamps and envelopes in a safety deposit box.

Make your collection less attractive to thieves by marking every album page with some identification. You can purchase a small rubber stamp that will do the job nicely and unobtrusively on the back or in the margin of each album page. Use your name and address or your name and telephone or stamp club membership number. Having identification on every page will assist in the documentation and recovery of the material if the robber attempts to sell it. If a valuable collection is ever stolen, notify the police and major stamp collecting organizations as quickly as possible.

## Children, family members, and pets

Small children are attracted to the bright colors and pretty pictures found in stamp albums. Children love to draw and color in books with their crayons and markers. You can be pretty sure they will want to play with any stamps they can get into their little hands and mouths. The simplest way to avoid this kind of damage is to put your stamps out of the reach of inquisitive children until they are old enough to handle them, and then spend some time enjoying your collection with your children.

Mint stamps have a host of problems related to keeping the gum pristine, but one not-so-well-known problem is that of uninformed family members mistaking a mint stamp for a collection as a mint stamp for letter mailing. Keep those stamps you intend to use as postage well away from any stamps for your collection. Inform your family members about what stamps they may use for ordinary postage.

Dogs and cats are especially fond of paper, including stamp collections. Dogs love chewing them. Cats are more partial to lying upon them, rolling around on them or chasing individual stamps across the floor with their claws extended. Avoid that damage by keeping albums and stamps on high shelves or in closets where pets cannot reach them.

ABOVE: Unsupervised infants and children can damage stamps. Illustrated is a 10 cent plus 5 cent semi-postal released by the Netherlands in 1947 to aid child welfare. BELOW: Dogs, such as those shown in a 1989 souvenir sheet from Finland, and other household pets can destroy stamp collections if left unattended.

# Preserving a Letter from Washington's

During the winter of 1777–1778, George Washington's army was encamped at Valley Forge, Pennsylvania, twenty miles outside of Philadelphia. Although we are taught in school about the sufferings and hardships endured during the bitter winter, we often forget how difficult it was to procure supplies during a time of war.

George Washington appointed Nathanael Greene as Quartermaster General at Valley Forge, charging him with obtaining supplies for the army. Greene wrote to merchant Joseph Webb, requesting portmanteaus (large, hinged suitcases), valises, and canvas for tents, knapsacks, and mattresses.

This folded letter is one of the treasures in the Smithsonian National Postal Museum's collection. It was sent on April 2, 1778, and franked "On publick Service," a typical marking for military mail sent for free through the Constitutional Post. The franking privilege is a practice dating to the seventeenth century that allows certain public offices to send official government correspondence for free. During wartime, soldiers can have their personal mail sent for free, as long as it is franked by an officer in charge.

The letter most likely traveled on a westerly route, starting in Valley Forge, heading north to Easton, Pennsylvania, on the Delaware River, and continuing

ABOVE LEFT: A conservator at the Smithsonian National Postal Museum flattens a crease in the Camp Valley Forge letter. ABOVE RIGHT: The conservator applies a mend to a tear in the letter. BOTTOM LEFT: The mend is dried. BOTTOM RIGHT: The mend is flattened. *All from the Smithsonian National Postal Museum conservation study collection.*

# Army at Camp Valley Forge

northeast to Fishkill, New York, and finally through Hartford, Connecticut, only three miles north of Wethersfield, Connecticut, its final destination.

Did you ever wonder why letters survive from two hundred years ago but modern photocopies look faded after only a few years? The answer is their relative rag content and the level of acidity. Colonial paper was often made out of cotton rags. Today, paper is usually made out of wood pulp, the processing of which results in highly acidic paper. The acidity causes the paper to turn yellow or brown and become brittle. The cellulose fibers break down, and the paper quickly deteriorates.

Despite the quality of the colonial paper, the Valley Forge letter still needed conservation treatment before it could go on exhibit. Conservation is the active approach to stabilizing artifacts using reversible techniques. The conservator flattened the creases as needed for stabilization of the artifact and for mending purposes. She then mended the tears and holes, filling any loss areas with

Japanese tissue paper applied with wheat starch paste. Any extraneous pencil notations made by previous collectors that were not original to the document were noted in the conservation report and then erased.

—Allison Marsh, Assistant Curator, National Postal Museum

A folded letter sent from Revolutionary War Camp Valley Forge by Nathanael Greene, Quartermaster General, on April 2, 1778. *From the Smithsonian National Postal Museum conservation study collection.*

## Natural disasters

Storms, floods, earthquakes, volcanic eruptions, tsunamis, and other natural disasters are the most difficult disasters for which to prepare. If you live in areas prone to natural disasters, make your stamp collection a part of your disaster plan. If you can evacuate, take the collection with you. If you cannot take it with you, try to find a protected place for the collection.

## Storage hazards

Use storage materials that are labeled "archival quality" or safe for long-term storage, but this advice does not carry over to any kind of albums designated "magnetic." These albums are designed to hold photographs. They are not even very safe for photographs, nor are they safe for anything else. Do not use them for any part of your stamp collection.

If you purchase stamps from a postal administration and they are sent to you in envelopes that have been marked as not being safe for permanent storage, believe them. Remove the stamps from these temporary containers and put them in albums or polyester sleeves.

Accidents are going to happen occasionally no

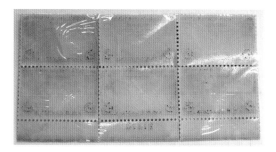

Some stamps may be purchased in shrink wrapping. If not removed, the wrapping continues to shrink and damages the contents. *From the Smithsonian National Postal Museum conservation study collection.*

matter how hard you work to avoid them, but there is no excuse for outright carelessness. Treat your stamps with care, and they will give you a lifetime of pleasure in return.

## Soaking and Hinge Removal Techniques
### Soaking stamps to remove them from envelopes

It is likely that some of the first stamps you will acquire for your collection will be taken from your own mail. Removing stamps from envelopes without damaging them is one of the first skills every stamp collector needs to learn.

Before removing stamps from envelopes, ascertain that no compelling reasons exist to leave them "on cover." (See Chapter Six, "Soak or save? When to keep the stamp on the envelope.") Use scissors to clip around the stamps. Leave at least a quarter inch of envelope paper all around so that the perforations are not clipped.

Safely removing the stamps from the paper will require soaking them in warm water. The temptation is strong to grab a handful of stamps and dunk them in a container of water, but this would be the worst thing you could do.

Sort the "on paper" stamps into several smaller groups before beginning the soaking process. Today a large proportion of stamps are self-adhesive. That means you peel them from self release paper and apply them to a letter or parcel. They require no moisture to activate the gum. Most self-adhesive stamps can be removed from paper by soaking in a water bath, but they take longer. It may be helpful to sort self-adhesive stamps from stamps with traditional water-activated gum, but it is not a problem if some self-adhesive stamps are mixed with water-activated gummed stamps on the same envelope. It will just require more careful monitoring.

That is your first sort, resulting in two groups of stamps. Each of those two groups of stamps should be sorted again into smaller groups: those stamps on white paper, stamps on colored paper, and stamps that have color cancels that might bleed and should be handled separately. Use this opportunity to remove and discard any stamps that are torn, heavily creased, or otherwise damaged. If there are many stamps to be soaked, you might want to separate them further by country of issue.

Stamps on colored paper are a problem because when subjected to moisture, the paper of many colored envelopes will bleed dye all over any stamps in the water. All colors may run, but the worst offenders are bright red and green envelopes commonly used to carry festive Christmas greetings. The red and green papers almost always bleed color when wet. The safest thing to do with stamps on any intensely colored envelopes is to throw them away or leave them on the envelope.

If you feel you must soak stamps from a colored envelope, then do so by soaking one at a time and change the water between soakings or use running water. You still might end up with a stamp that has been colored bright red or green, but you will have only ruined one stamp, not a whole batch.

Treat stamps on manila envelopes as though they are on colored paper. Sometimes coloring agents in manila paper will bleed. It is not possible to tell which manila paper will bleed by looking at it, so play it safe and soak them separately. Cut the colored borders from airmail envelope clippings, too, because sometimes those colored diagonal lozenges bleed. Soak these separately, too, if it is not possible to trim away the colored border without damaging the stamp.

Use care with colored or heavy cancels and treat them as though they were on colored paper. Some of the red-ink circular datestamp cancels used by the United States Postal Service may run and bleed. Use caution when soaking all stamps that were canceled by handstamps. As a rule of thumb, most machine cancels are stable. Cancels made by handstamps, which often use red or purple ink, may not be stable. With practice and experience, you will be able to pick out the cancels that will cause problems when soaking.

Sort out stamps that have holographic images as part of their designs. Sometimes these foil-based printed images flake, peel, or float free from the stamp when soaked in water.

Fill a large bowl with warm water and work with small numbers of stamps. The biggest mistake some collectors make is filling a sink full of water and dumping in a huge lot of stamps. Do not do that. If stamps stay in the water too long, they lose their sizing and can begin to break down into a soggy pulp. It will be impossible to remove the stamps quickly enough if there are too many in the water at one time, so work in batches of not more than 50 stamps at one time. Change the water in the bowl before doing another batch of stamps.

Immerse the stamps in the water and wait for them to release. As soon as a stamp floats free from the paper, remove it from the water, rinse it and place it face down on a thin, old (but clean) bath towel that is reserved just for stamp drying. Some people prefer to use paper towels or newspaper for

## Don't Sweat! Use a Sweatbox Instead.

What should you do with those great-looking holo-gram stamps? You can always try floating them on top of the water in your soaking bowl. The objective is to get the backing paper wet but to keep the stamp itself as dry as possible.

You also can attempt using a "**sweatbox**." A sweatbox is a sealed container that provides a very humid environment for stamps that are exposed to it. The humidity softens the gum, making it possible to remove the stamp from the paper without soaking the stamp. Sweatboxes are commercially available, but you can make your own. You will need a clean plastic container with a tight-fitting lid and a sponge. Put a half-inch of water in the bottom of the container. Put the sponge in the water and allow it to draw up some of the moisture. Then put the stamp on top of the sponge and put the lid on the container.

It may take several hours or even several days for the stamp to release, but there is much less chance of damaging the hologram or detaching it from the rest of the stamp. When the stamp releases from the paper, move it to the stamp-drying book. This method works best with traditional water-activated gum and it is good to use a sweatbox for older stamps that have been on piece for a long time.

A sweatbox is useful to remove a hinge that won't peel or a mint stamp that is stuck flat on an album page. If the stamp is unused and you want to try to save the gum, you need to use a sweatbox. After several hours or more in the sweatbox, the gum on the hinge should have softened enough for you to be able to peel it off by using stamp tongs to get a grip on one corner of the hinge remnant. Dry the stamp as previously explained.

Some of the gum will be lost by this method, and all of it will be damaged, so the best that you can hope for is retaining part of the original gum, but you have saved a stamp that can fill a space in your album until a better example comes along.

this step, but a bath towel works best and can be washed and reused indefinitely.

Take your time. Tears and thins will almost certainly result if you attempt to help the soaking process along by pulling the stamps from the backing paper before they are ready to release on their own. Do not start soaking unless you have enough time to do the job properly.

The stamps will begin to curl as they dry. To counteract the curling, move the stamps to a drying book just before they are completely dry. Drying books are commercially available, but you can make your own. The books consist of several pages of blotting paper interleaved with sheets of plastic. You place the nearly dry stamps face up on the plastic page, and place the blotting page down on top of the stamps. Keep the drying book flat and place a heavy book on top of it for a day or two. The stamps will then be dry, almost always wrinkle free, and ready to be mounted in your album or placed in a stock book.

If you lack a drying book, remove the stamps from the towel and spread them on blotting paper, leaving enough space between them so that they don't touch each other. Put another piece of blotting paper on top of the stamps, or use waxed paper if it appears there are any traces of gum left on any of the stamps. The stamps will not stick to the waxed paper as they dry. Put several heavy books on top of the final layer of blotting paper or waxed paper.

The stamps will be free from paper, flat, and dry in several hours. When they are completely dry the stamps may be mounted in an album or put away in stock books.

Many collectors complain about self-adhesive stamps, but most are not as problematic as some make them out to be. Self-adhesives are convenient and popular with the general public, so they will constitute an increasingly large percentage of the stamps you will soak for your collection.

Most self-adhesives from the United States soak nearly as well as stamps with water-activated gum, but some self-adhesives require a little extra nudging. Some of them come away from their backing paper cleanly, but they require a little tug at the corner of the stamp to get them started. Just bend the paper to which they are affixed away from the stamp and lift the stamp off. If the stamp does not slip easily away from the paper, return it to the water and give it more time soaking before trying the procedure again.

Occasionally the adhesive will stick firmly to the backs of some self-adhesive stamps, even after removing most of the remaining envelope. In these instances the sticky stuff will usually come off by holding the stamp under water and very gently rubbing the adhesive off with your finger. This takes some time and a gentle touch, but it works.

Unfortunately there are a small number of self-adhesives that are a soaking disaster. The adhesive sticks firmly to the back of the stamp and will not come off even with the rubbing technique just mentioned. The best way to save these stamps is mint on their original peelable backing or on the paper envelope fragment that has been closely clipped.

### Removing hinges from the backs of stamps

Stamp hinges do not always peel cleanly from the backs of stamps. Good hinging techniques (see Chapter 4, "Hinges and mounts") can minimize the problem, but not always.

**Methyl cellulose**—Some museums use methyl cellulose to remove stubborn hinges from stamps. This product is available from archival suppliers (see Chapter Ten, "Sources") and has the advantage of not saturating the stamps completely as water would. Methyl cellulose is a powder that must be mixed with warm water (2 teaspoons of methyl cellulose mixed in 1½ cups of warm water). The mixture should sit for several minutes until it becomes gel-like.

Gather a small amount of the gel on an artist's paintbrush and apply it to the back of the hinge. Begin from the center of the hinge and evenly apply the gel out to the edges. This will help eliminate the back of the stamp from warping and will make the hinge easier to remove.

When the hinge appears to look saturated (wait at least thirty seconds to absorb) you can often remove the hinge with one swoop of the tongs. If the hinge breaks down, allow the methyl cellulose to dry and apply another coat to the remnants. It is good to practice on very common stamps before you attempt using methyl cellulose on an expensive stamp.

**Soaking**—If the stamp with a stuck hinge is postally used, the hinge will float free after a quick soak in water.

If the stamp is unused with original gum, allow it to dry completely before attempting removal. After it has dried, try to pull the hinge from the back of the stamp. If it does not pull easily and cleanly away from the stamp, do not force it. You can use an artist's paintbrush to apply a little water to the hinge remnant and remove it when the gum on the hinge softens.

### CHAPTER EIGHT

# IS IT GENUINE AND WHAT IS IT WORTH?

## Is It Genuine?

Most worldwide stamp collections contain at least a few forged or faked stamps. This is inevitable because forgeries are far more plentiful than genuine examples in some cases. The stamps may have been forged to fool a stamp collector or to swindle a postal administration from its rightful fee for providing a service. In either instance, the net result is the same—a stamp collection ends up sheltering an item that is not what it is purported to be.

Fakes and forgeries can be collectible in their own right. Removing forgeries from an album and assembling them into a separate collection is an excellent learning opportunity. A stamp collector armed with knowledge can avoid paying for a genuine stamp and receiving a forgery instead.

## Forgeries, Fakes, Counterfeits, and Bogus Stamps—Are They the Same?

Stamp collectors will encounter several terms that are often used indiscriminately and interchangeably to describe stamps or covers that are not genuine. These terms are not exactly the same.

A **forgery** is an imitation of a genuine stamp, overprint, surcharge, postal marking, or cancellation. The term includes **postal forgeries** designed to cheat the post office and

OPPOSITE: Detail of 1907 stamp from Solomon Islands.

# Do-It-Yourself Forgery Detection

Two stamps from the British Solomon Islands are illustrated here. One is a forgery. Can you tell which one?

Both stamps show a native war canoe and are crudely printed by lithography. Both stamps are canceled. The *Scott Catalogue* states "counterfeits are plentiful" in a footnote below the listing for these two stamps. That signals the alert.

*Stanley Gibbons British Commonwealth Stamp Catalogue* goes a bit farther, stating "forgeries show different perforations and have the boat paddle touching the shore. Genuine stamps show a gap between the paddle and the shore."

That is useful information, but if you have nothing to compare you might wonder what is meant by "the shore" and which paddle they are talking about.

This is where additional reference works are useful in determining whether the stamps are genuine or forgeries. One source is *British Solomon Islands* by Harold G. D. Gisburne (published 1956 in Great Britain). Gisburne states that genuine stamps have perforations that gauge 11 and the bow paddle does not touch the shore in the foreground. The perforations on the forgeries gauge 11½ and the bow paddle touches the shore. He further states there are a number of minor differences, and that "used" copies

of the forgeries can be found having a bogus "Munia" postmark.

A second reference is *Billig's Philatelic Handbook* (Vol. II, published 1943, Jamaica, New York) that graphically illustrates the differences between the genuine and the forged 1907 British Solomon Islands large canoe issue.

Now that you are armed with knowledge and facts about the stamps, can you tell which one is genuine and which is a forgery?

Measuring the perforations using a perforation gauge is a simple matter. The 6d stamp has perforations that gauge 11 ½ and the paddle at the canoe's bow (on the right side of the stamp) touches the shore. The cancel is bogus. The 1 shilling stamp has perforations that gauge 11 and the paddle does not touch the shoreline just above the 1 shilling value tablet at the lower right. The cancel is genuine. The 6d stamp is a forgery (the paddle touches the shore). The 1 shilling stamp is genuine.

Having the right reference book at hand is crucial for work such as this, but many excellent philatelic reference books are out of print. Philatelic libraries and philatelic literature dealers are excellent sources for these works. (See Chapter Ten, "Sources.")

Two 1907 stamps from Solomon Islands. One is genuine and one is a forgery. Which one is which? Sidebar text has the answer.

LEFT: A bogus stamp is not based on any known design and has never been issued by a postal administration. This "stamp" inscribed Tonga was never issued by Tonga. RIGHT: A genuine 1923 2 pence on 10 pence stamp from Tonga that has a fake Nuku'alofa postmark of a type and size never used in Tonga.

philatelic forgeries designed to cheat stamp collectors. The word "counterfeit" is used interchangeably with "forgery."

A bogus stamp, postmark, or cover is a complete fabrication, perhaps designed to fool a stamp collector, but based on no known genuine example.

Genuine stamps and covers can be faked. This means they have been altered or tampered with in some way to trick collectors into believing they are more valuable or desirable. Overprints, surcharges, perforations, cancellations, and gum have all been faked on stamps.

Reprints and facsimiles can also deceive stamp collectors. Reprints are usually made by or with the authorization of postal authorities. The stamps are printed from the original plates and often in the original colors. These can make identification quite tricky. Reprints can also be faked by adding perforations, reperforating, rebacking with a new paper backing that has a different watermark, or any number of other changes designed for deception.

Facsimiles are much less troublesome. Facsimilies are made to look like a genuine stamp but are not printed from the original plates. They often differ considerably from the stamp they are trying to imitate and there has been no intent by its creator to defraud.

Stamp collectors have the most problems with

Two stamps purporting to be "North West Pacific Islands" overprints. The genuine (right) example shows crisp serifs (straight lines) on the ends of the letters. The letters are rounded on the fake (left).

fakes and forgeries, both of which can and have been done by highly skilled experts whose intention it is to sell the items to collectors.

Many forgeries can be discovered by ordinary stamp collectors who are diligent in their collecting habits. Other stamps and covers have been so skillfully forged or faked that more assistance is needed. Fortunately there are expertizing services that stand ready to assist collectors. (See Chapter Ten, "Sources.")

## First Steps to Detecting Forgeries and Fakes

A stamp catalog is worth its weight in gold when it comes to detecting fakes and forgeries. For example, the *Scott Standard Postage Stamp Catalogues* print warnings alerting collectors to be cautious regarding issues that have been forged or faked. Phrases such as "dangerous counterfeits exist," "counterfeits are plentiful," or "beware of fake cancellations," are peppered throughout *Scott Catalogues* and serve as friendly advice when acquiring stamps for your collection.

When these kinds of notations appear in a catalog, take a good look at the stamps you already have. The catalogs usually will not advise a collector how to tell the good from the bad, but checking specialized handbooks and reference works will assist in separating philatelic wheat from chaff.

Review the listing for the stamp or stamps under suspicion. Check for a watermark. A good clue you may not have a genuine stamp is if the stamp should have a watermark and there is none. Is it the correct watermark? Look carefully at the paper with a good magnifier. Stamps can be rebacked to give the appearance of the correct watermark. A close inspection may be able to distinguish this kind of fakery as well as reveal any thins or defects in the stamp.

Verify the method of printing. If the stamp is listed as being engraved and the one you have is lithographed, then you have either checked the wrong listing for a similar-looking stamp, or your stamp may not be genuine.

Look at the perforations and measure their gauge. The gauge of perforations is more easily faked than printing or watermarks. Perforations may be added to a straight edge or to a wide margin of an off-center to improve the appearance of a stamp. Stamps can also be reperforated in a scarcer gauge to trick a buyer into paying much more for it. When looking at perforations, check to see that the holes on all sides match in appearance and that holes on one side are parallel to those on the opposite side. The tips of a reperforated stamp that has had a straight edge will often still be straight and crisp, unlike the feathery tips of perforations that have been torn naturally when separating one stamp from another.

Gum may be added to used stamps that have not been canceled or that have had the cancel chemically cleaned. This will give a used stamp the appearance of a mint stamp that may be significantly more valuable. The liquid gum may pool around the perforation holes and cover the feathery tips of the perforations during the regumming process and remain visible when the gum has dried. Look for these telltale signs of regumming before paying a lot more for a mint stamp with full original gum.

Cancels can be removed or added to a stamp. Pen cancels are fairly easy to remove, although almost always a trace of the cancel will remain. Using an ultraviolet light will sometimes bring out the faded cancel, but not always. Some stamps are more valuable if they are canceled, and some scarce cancels are valuable even if found on very common stamps. Knowing the characteristics of the kinds of cancels likely to be found on any particular stamp is the best way to avoid paying too much for a scarce cancel.

Surcharges and overprints are easy to fake, but even these have their own characteristics. Know the kind of printing method that was used to create the surcharge or overprint and check that the printing method is correct. Consult a catalog to ascertain what lettering or illustration should have been used on the stamp. The overprint should match the illustration.

Inks used to print a stamp can be altered chemically or photochemically. Colors can also be faded so as to appear missing altogether. If considering the purchase of an expensive "missing color" or "wrong color" stamp, it is best to have it certified as genuine by a reputable expertizing service.

Covers are sometimes faked to become more desirable to collectors. Stamps that were not there originally can be added. Scarce postal markings can also be added, or postal markings already on the cover can be altered to become more aesthetically pleasing. Learn as much as you can about rates, the proper stamps utilized to pay those rates, and the postal markings used at the time. This is the very best defense against buying a faked cover.

Knowledge is the power that protects you from buying faked or forged material. Fortunately, there are many good references on the subject of philatelic fakes and forgeries. (See Chapter Ten, "Sources.")

## Getting an Expert's Opinion

Several excellent expertizing services write certificates that will verify stamps or covers as genuine or counterfeit. Fees for this service start at around thirty dollars and escalate according to the catalog value of the item being examined. Forms for submitting items to be expertized are available by writing the service or downloading the form from their website. Read the instructions carefully before submitting any item.

You will be asked to provide a brief description of the item and its catalog number. You also have to submit the item for examination using a secure method of delivery. (The submission form will advise you how to submit the item.) You will be asked what information about the item you are seeking. Generally, you will want to know whether the item is genuine and properly identified. You also may request an opinion on whether it has been repaired or altered.

The expertizing service will have at least one and usually several experts examine and render an opinion about the item you submitted. The item you submitted will be returned with a certificate that bears a photograph of the item along with the opinion of the expertizers, who could determine that the item was genuine, counterfeit, or that they were unable to render an opinion. The certificate will enumerate any faults or condition problems. Some expertizing services will give a numerical score indicative of the stamp's grade.

If you plan to submit an item you are considering purchasing for expertizing, contact the seller or auction firm first. Often dealers and auction houses have specific procedures that must be

One cent stamp expertized as genuine by the American
Philatelic Society's Expertizing Service (APEX).

followed for items sold pending the outcome of a "good" (genuine) expert opinion. Check first to avoid later complications.

Spend a little money to have a stamp or cover expertized if you have doubts about whether it is genuine. It could save you thousands of dollars lost by an uninformed purchase of a fake or forgery.

## How Much Is It Worth? Factors Affecting Stamp Value

The "how much is it worth?" question seems to follow stamp collectors wherever they go. Many people believe that an old stamp is worth a lot of money just because it is old. But stamp values actually depend on many variables.

### Supply and demand

Stamps, like other goods, are priced according to the law of supply and demand. If the supply exceeds the demand, the price usually will decrease. If the demand exceeds supply, prices normally rise. Other factors that affect stamp values are the cost of doing business and the ability of the marketplace to purchase the goods. These are the same market conditions that affect other types of goods, but with stamps there is one difference. Stamps are not an essential purchase, so demand is really the key variable.

Demand for stamps can change as collecting habits change. Some countries or types of stamps will become popular for a time and then fall out of favor with stamp collectors. During the period of high popularity, prices may soar as demand exceeds supply. When the bubble bursts and the demand is no longer present, there may be a glut of this material in the marketplace and prices will fall accordingly.

## Condition and grade

Supply and demand are better-known market variables, but condition and grade eclipse them for all kinds of collectibles. This is true with stamps, too, although supply and demand can overrule condition when a stamp in poor condition is unique or known to exist only in poor condition.

Condition refers to the physical state of the stamp. Common stamps in damaged condition will have no resale value. A stamp that has tears or scuffing; is cut-to-shape; is soiled, stained or faded; is creased, thinned, or has missing or damaged perforations is a damaged stamp.

An unused stamp should have full original gum for it to be considered in the most desirable condition possible. Many collectors will pay a premium for stamps with full original gum that have not been hinged. Used stamps in general should be lightly canceled.

Gum may sometimes cause damage to a stamp, especially an older unused stamp, over time. Gum is not always stable. It can warp, crack, shrink, and discolor. Removing the gum from an unused stamp sounds counterintuitive, especially when factoring the difference in value for unused stamps with original gum. However, it may be more important to conserve the appearance of the front of a valuable stamp that is developing gum problems than to conserve the gum. A stamp with cracked gum will eventually break along the cracks. The original gum will not be of much use or value at that point.

Stamp collectors and dealers use many terms to describe various factors that affect condition. Abbreviations for some of these terms appear in auction catalogs and price lists. Get to know the terms before buying, because any condition issues will affect a stamp's value.

### Condition terminology

***Pulled perf, pulled perforation*** A perforation that is shorter than it should be, through careless separation from a pane of stamps or through mishandling by a collector.

An 85 franc waterbuck stamp issued by Senegal in 1960 shows a pulled perforation at the top left.

The back of a 1913 stamp from Ivory Coast that shows thinning caused by humidity making the stamp stick to an album page. When pulled from the page, part of it stayed affixed.

**Thin** A skimming of paper upon which the stamp is printed. This usually occurs on the reverse of the stamp when a stamp hinge has been improperly removed, but a thin may naturally occur during the manufacture of paper.

**Inclusion** A flaw within the paper that occurred during manufacture.

**Tear** A split or rip in the paper. These are generally reported in price lists by the degree of severity.

**Blunt perfs, nibbed perfs** Perforations that have been rounded, usually through age or use, but sometimes through mishandling.

**Blunt corner** A corner of stamp or cover that is rounded rather than crisp and straight.

**Skim, scuff** An abrasion that occurs on the front of a stamp or cover.

**Fading** Exposure to light or chemicals will fade inks used to print a stamp.

**Oxidation** Change of color due to aging or exposure to chemicals or fumes. Some colors, such as orange, are more prone to oxidation than others. Orange stamps will often oxidize and turn brown.

LEFT: The top of this 1956 ½ penny stamp from Jamaica shows perforations that were blunted because the stamp was put in a stamp mount that was too small for the stamp. RIGHT: The top left corner of this 1948 40 centimes stamp from Ruanda Urundi exhibits a blunt corner at the top left.

**Foxing** Brown or rust-colored spots on paper. The exact cause of foxing is not known but it is believed to be a combination of age and a fungus that is partial to some kinds of machine-made paper. Foxing can be minimized by storing paper materials (including stamps) within optimal climate parameters.

**Original gum** The condition of gum on the stamp as it was immediately after production. There are no hinge marks, missing gum, or damage from moisture. The abbreviation "OG" is often used.

**Disturbed gum** Gum that has been marred by a hinge that has been removed or shows evidence of having been moistened, stuck down, or otherwise impaired.

**Hinged** Stamps that have had a stamp hinge applied to it are thereafter known as hinged. If the stamp has been hinged more than once it may be called "heavily hinged," often abbreviated as "HH." If the hinge has been properly applied and then removed completely leaving no residue, it is said to be "lightly hinged," often abbreviated as "LH." A mint stamp that has never been hinged and has its full original gum is often referred to as "never hinged" and is abbreviated as "NH." The term "unmounted" is used in the United Kingdom and some other countries and has the same meaning as "never hinged."

With covers, condition usually means looking for those that are not faded, torn, stained, folded, or otherwise damaged. Cancels on covers should be neat and readable and are best when they "tie" the stamps to the envelopes—that is, when the cancel strikes both the stamp and the envelope.

Of course, there are exceptions. Crash covers, redirected and returned mail, or envelopes that have been subjected to other than ordinary mailing conditions are expected to show evidence of their journeys. They usually are more collectible because they have endured extraordinary circumstances.

### Grades

Grade refers to how well a stamp is centered. Collectors need to understand grading before buying stamps—especially very expensive stamps. A badly centered stamp such as the one illustrated on page 124 will have a fraction of the value of one that is centered with the same or nearly the same margins all around the stamp.

Poorly centered stamps have perforations that cut into the design. Stamps with average centering have perforations touch but not infringe on the design. Stamps with fine centering are noticeably off-center on two sides. These grades of poor, average, and fine are worth only fractions of their catalog values. Stamps in the grade of very fine (almost on-center on one side or slightly off-center on two sides) can be expected to sell at retail for about catalog value. Stamps in the grade of extremely fine (close to perfectly centered) can be expected to sell for more than their catalog value, as can stamps in the grade of superb (perfectly centered).

Stamp collectors are used to referring to the grade of stamps by using the descriptions of poor,

ABOVE LEFT: A United States 1861 3 cent Washington stamp with average (AVG) centering. ABOVE RIGHT: A United States 1894 1 cent Franklin showing average to fine (AVG-F) centering. BOTTOM LEFT: A United States 1873 3 cent Washington stamp with very fine (VF) centering. BOTTOM RIGHT: A United States 1894 2 cent Washington with extremely fine (XF) centering.

average, fine, very fine, extremely fine, and superb. Some expertizing services that authenticate stamps are now issuing certificates of genuineness that use numerical grade for stamps. (See "Sources," Chapter Ten.) The time-honored advice about buying the best grade of stamp that you can afford remains valid.

Grade is mostly an issue in stamps of the classic period—that is, stamps issued in the nineteenth century. Given modern production capabilities, expect most modern stamps to be fine–very fine or better.

Factor in the popularity of a collecting area. Some stamps, countries, and time periods are more popular with collectors than others. Popularity of collecting areas waxes and wanes just as it does in all other areas of taste and preference.

The popularity variable can work to the advantage of budget-minded collectors.

You can get more bang for your hobby bucks if you pick a country or subject that is not presently popular. Over time what you collect might become more popular, but you should also realize that you run the risk of assembling a collection that might have little marketability. If you are enjoying assembling your collection now, that should not make a lot of difference. There is value in fun.

## So How Much Is It *Really* Worth?

All these variables affect the value of stamps and covers, but has the question, "How much it is worth" been answered? That depends on what you mean by "worth."

If you need to know the value of your collection for insurance purposes, then that would be the replacement value—how much it would cost to replace the collection should it become lost, stolen, or otherwise destroyed.

If you are planning to sell your collection, you need the appraised cash value. Always remember that a stamp dealer expects to make a profit from reselling your stamps in order to stay in business. He cannot do that by buying your stamps at full catalog value. Neither the replacement value nor the appraised cash value correlate exactly to catalog value, which is simply a guide that takes into consideration all of the variables of supply, demand, grade, condition, and popularity.

Stamps sell substantially below or, more uncommonly, above catalog values, depending on all of the variables. There really is no simple answer to the question "How much is it worth?" That always depends on how much another collector is willing to pay to acquire it for their collection.

The bottom line is this: Buy the best quality you can afford and take good care of your stamp collection. You will be able to recover at least some or maybe all of the money you put into the collection when it comes time to sell. If all of the factors that affect the stamp market are favorable, you might even make a profit. However, you cannot put a dollar value on the friends you make, the knowledge you gain, the stress you relieve, the fun you had, the thrills you get, or the satisfaction your collection provides. Those additional benefits make your stamp collection priceless.

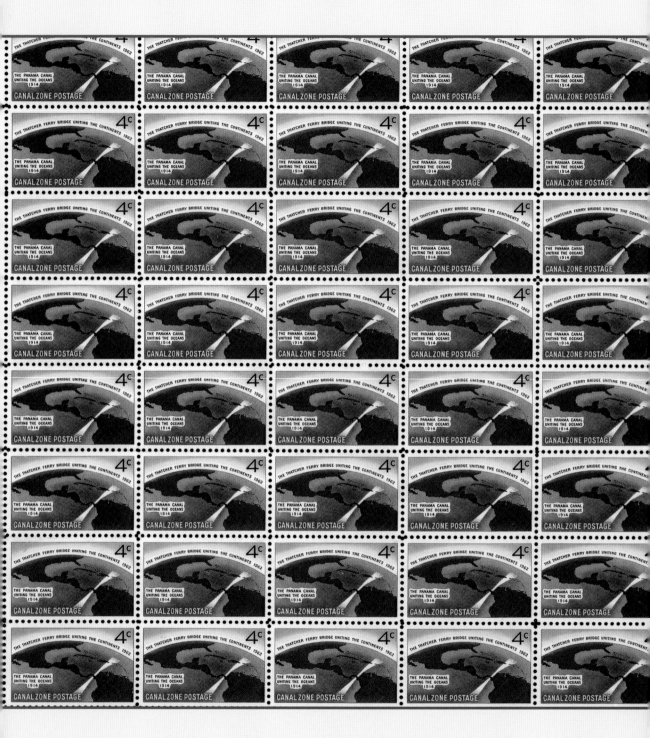

### CHAPTER NINE

# STAMPS OF DISTINCTION

## Treasures from the Smithsonian National Postal Museum

The Smithsonian National Postal Museum opened on July 30, 1993 in the historic Old City Post Office Building directly across from Union Station in Washington, D.C. It houses one of the largest stamp collections in the world, but the museum is more than just a "stamp museum."

The National Postal Museum's galleries entertain and educate visitors on subjects as varied as the way development of transportation affected the delivery of mail and how an ever-improving postal system aided the expansion and growth of the United States. The philatelic gallery displays some of the finest collections ever assembled. The National Postal Museum provides interactive fun and programs for the whole family, and it is a palace of endless delights for a stamp collector.

Although the National Postal Museum is one of the smallest of the Smithsonian museums in physical size, it has one of the largest collections of objects. Only a very small percentage of the stamps, covers, and postal artifacts can be displayed within the confines of the National Postal Museum at any one time.

OPPOSITE: Detail of a pane of the 1962 Canal Zone "missing Thatcher Bridge" stamps. *From the Smithsonian National Postal Museum collection.*

# The First U.S. Postage Stamp

Rawdon, Wright, Hatch, and Edson, a banknote engraving firm, prepared the essays (or trial designs for the proposed postage stamp) for the first United States general issue of postage stamps. Postmaster General Cave Johnson initially instructed the firm to use a portrait of recently deceased President Andrew Jackson on the 5 cent stamp and George Washington on the 10 cent denomination. However, the essay, drawn in India ink and pencil, showed that Jackson had been replaced by Benjamin Franklin, who was the first postmaster general appointed under the Continental Congress.

Franklin's portrait, based on artwork by James B. Longacre, would be more acceptable as a unifying icon for the divided nation because of his role in securing independence for the country. Both the Franklin and Washington stamps became valid for use on July 1, 1847. The 5 cent Franklin stamp paid the rate for a half-ounce letter sent less than 300 miles.

The city of Philadelphia appointed Franklin, who operated a print shop there, its postmaster general in 1737. This role increased his newspaper's paid advertisements and circulation, because Franklin could distribute his gazette free of charge. Franklin admitted in his autobiography that, in earlier times, he had bribed riders to carry his papers privately and "out of the mails" (outside the official postal system). In his new role as postmaster, he sought more efficient, reliable, and profitable operations. Then in 1753 the British government appointed him joint deputy postmaster for the colonies. His efforts

ABOVE: The United States's first stamp, a 5 cent value showing the portrait of Benjamin Franklin. BOTTOM: An essay of the 5 cent Franklin stamp that was rendered in India ink and pencil. *Both images from the Smithsonian National Postal Museum collection.*

# Honored Benjamin Franklin

extended mail delivery outside the colonies, initiated night travel for postal riders to speed delivery, and created a dead letter office for undeliverable mail. By 1757 he had surveyed the post roads and reorganized postal operations, a step that allowed smoother communication among the colonies—which was ultimately crucial to the Revolution.

In 1774 the British displaced Franklin as postmaster but allowed him the right to mail letters free of postage. To take advantage of this privilege, Franklin was to inscribe the outside of the letter "Free," followed by his name. According to some sources, Franklin used this free franking privilege to convey a message of patriotism. Instead of "Free B. Franklin," he began to sign "B. Free Franklin." In 1775 Franklin became a Pennsylvania delegate to the Second Continental Congress, which appointed him the first postmaster general of the independent united colonies, a position he held until he left to serve as ambassador to France in 1776.

*—Cheryl R. Ganz, Curator of Philately,
National Postal Museum*

A letter sent from the printers, Rawdon Wright, to the office of the postmaster general regarding the Franklin essay. *From the Smithsonian National Postal Museum collection.*

ABOVE: Benjamin Franklin's free frank, used on a folded letter sent to John Hancock. RIGHT: Franklin later changed his free frank to "B. Free Franklin." *Both images from the Smithsonian National Postal Museum collection.*

The famous "inverted Jenny" 24 cent 1918 United States airmail stamp with an inverted center. *From the Smithsonian National Postal Museum collection.*

Here are some of the curators' favorites from the National Postal Museum collection. To see more, visit the Smithsonian National Postal Museum in person at 2 Massachusetts Avenue, N.E., Washington, DC 20002 or online at www.postalmuseum.si.edu.

### Everybody's Favorite: The United States 24 Cent "Inverted Jenny"

A printing mistake occasionally turns a common stamp into a highly prized trophy. Arguably, the 1918 24 cent airmail stamp with an inverted center is the most famous and recognizable United States stamp. An unused regular copy of the stamp is worth something less than one hundred dollars in today's market. A stamp of the same issue with an inverted center can be sold for two thousand times that price. Only one sheet of one hundred of these stamps, affectionately known as the Inverted Jenny, was sold. The lucky buyer was William T. Robey of Washington, D.C.

Inverted stamp errors are created when a sheet of stamps passes through more than one printing, usually to add another color. If one sheet has been turned around while being moved when the sheets are set up for the second pass, the frame or vignette will print upside down. In the case of the Inverted Jenny, the frame could have been printed first. Then one sheet may have been inadvertently turned around when the center vignette was printed. Thus the completed stamp showed the plane flying upside down in relation to the frame.

### Kingdom of Hawaii Missionary Cover

The strip of three 13 cent stamps shown here is the only known multiple of the exceedingly rare "Hawaiian missionaries" stamps—postage stamps issued by the kingdom of Hawaii in the early 1850s that American missionaries often used. The envelope was badly damaged by fire. It was found in a New York furnace where trash had been burned. The Hawaiian missionary cover has been extensively repaired to compensate for the fire damage. Who knows what other gems were lost forever to this fire?

This extensively repaired cover bears a strip of three exceedingly rare 13 cent Hawaiian missionary stamps. It was burned with other trash in a furnace in New York. *From the Smithsonian National Postal Museum collection.*

Cover from Wells Fargo Virginia City Pony Service that ran between San Francisco, Sacramento, Carson City, and Virginia City in Nevada. *From the Smithsonian National Postal Museum collection.*

## Wells Fargo "Virginia City Pony" Express Cover

Illustrated here is an early use of the 1862–1865 Wells, Fargo and Company service—also referred to as the "Virginia City Pony" service—which ran from San Francisco via Sacramento and Carson City to Virginia City, Nevada. This service was different from the short-lived transcontinental Pony Express. It specialized in the quick delivery of important business letters and newspapers between the gold and silver mining areas of Nevada and California business centers. This piece was created by pasting the front top portion of a 3 cent 1861 stamped envelope onto the front of a plain envelope. It also bears the 25 cent 1862 Wells Fargo stamp and the company's blue cancel postmarked Virginia City, Nevada Territory.

## Mailing the Priceless and Legendary Hope Diamond

Beautiful and dangerous, with a lurid past as stormy as the queens who once wore it, the Hope diamond at the Smithsonian's Museum of Natural History is almost a compulsory stop on the family visit to Washington D.C. The National Postal Museum has the package in which it was mailed to the Smithsonian.

The Hope diamond's cursed reputation is as well known as the gem. The diamond gets its name from London banker Henry T. Hope, who purchased it in 1839. After Hope's death, the diamond passed through the hands of various owners.

Mrs. Evalyn Walsh McLean, a Washington D.C. socialite and wife of the former owner of the *Washington Post*, acquired the diamond in 1911 for $180,000. She, too, suffered the curse of the diamond: Her husband died in a mental institution, her eldest son was killed in a car accident, and her daughter overdosed on sleeping pills. Although she believed in the curse, she continued to wear the diamond. Mrs. McLean would not sell it for fear

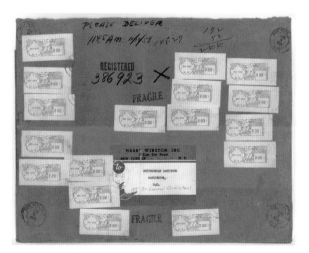

The parcel that contained the Hope diamond bore $145.29 in metered postage. Only $2.44 was for the postage; the remainder was for the $1 million value insurance fee. *From the Smithsonian National Postal Museum collection.*

of bringing the bad luck to someone else. After her death in 1947 the diamond was found, along with $4 million worth of other jewels, stored in shoeboxes in Mrs. McLean's bedroom.

Henry "Harry" Winston, a leading American jeweler and gem dealer, bought the diamond from Mrs. McLean's estate in 1949. In November 1958 Winston donated the diamond to the Smithsonian Institution, intending it to be the foundation for a National Jewel Collection. With his years of experience in shipping jewelry all over the world, Winston chose to have the diamond delivered by registered mail. He told a reporter for the *Washington Post* that "[Registered mail is] the safest way to ship gems. . . . I've sent gems all over the world that way."

The diamond was placed in a box, wrapped in brown paper, and sent by registered mail, traveling down from New York in a Railway Post Office train car. In Washington, it was immediately taken to the City Post Office (the building that now houses the National Postal Museum), where it was picked up by postal carrier James G. Todd.

Todd drove the package to the National Museum of Natural History. The diamond was handed over in a ceremony including Leonard Carmichael, Secretary of the Smithsonian Institution and Mrs. Harry Winston. The transfer was completed when Carmichael signed the receipt for the registered package. The price paid for shipping the gem, valued at $1 million at the time, was $145.29, most of that for package insurance.

## 1869 Inverted Centers

In 1869, a series of stamps was printed depicting American symbols and history. Three denominations of inverted stamps were mistakenly created during the production of this series. Inverts appeared in the 15 cent, 24 cent, and 30 cent issues.

Only about ninety used and three unused copies are recorded from the 15 cent issue. The central design illustrates the Landing of Columbus, originally engraved by John Balch.

Approximately eighty-four used and four unused copies have been recorded from the 24 cent issue. The vignette shows The Declaration of Independence, July 4, 1776 at Philadelphia, originally painted by John Trumbull.

Only about thirty-seven used and seven unused copies are recorded as still existing from the 30 cent issue. The central design of this stamp illustrates the American Eagle, Shield, and Flags, from a wash drawing by James Macdonough.

Inverted center on the 15 cent United States 1869 regular issue stamps. *From the Smithsonian National Postal Museum collection.*

LEFT: Inverted center on the 24 cent United States 1869 regular issue stamps. RIGHT: Inverted center on the 30 cent United States 1869 regular issue stamps. *Both images from the Smithsonian National Postal Museum collection.*

## 1919 Flying Boat Mail

The first piece of mail flown across the Atlantic was carried in 1919 on the NC-4, the U.S. Navy "Flying Boat" that successfully completed the first transatlantic flight. Before the flight, the plane and its crew were in Halifax, Canada. Machinist Pat Carroll wrote a letter to his brother Charles, a corporal with the American Expeditionary Forces in France. Pat asked a member of the NC-4 flight crew to carry the letter and mail it after the flight. The plane left Halifax on May 15, flying first to Trepassey, Newfoundland. The plane reached the Azores on May 20 and Lisbon, Portugal on May 27, where the letter was placed in the mail.

The first piece of mail flown across the Atlantic Ocean was addressed to a soldier with the American Expeditionary Forces in France in 1919. *From the Smithsonian National Postal Museum collection.*

## Canal Zone Thatcher Bridge Error

Inverted stamps are not the only valuable printing errors. Some of the 1962 Canal Zone stamps were issued with the Thatcher Bridge missing. One sheet of 200 stamps without the silver bridge escaped detection and was shipped to the Canal Zone Postal Administration. One pane of fifty stamps was sold to an American stamp dealer before the error was discovered. Of the three other panes recovered, two were donated to the National Postal Museum and the third was destroyed.

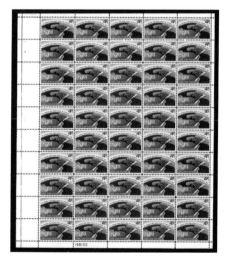

A complete pane of fifty of the 1962 Canal Zone "missing Thatcher Bridge" stamps. *From the Smithsonian National Postal Museum collection.*

## President Franklin Roosevelt, Stamp Designer

Franklin Delano Roosevelt was one of the most famous stamp collectors in the United States. As president, Roosevelt was in a unique position to indulge his love of stamps. One way he did that was to sketch his own design proposals for stamps.

Roosevelt's original sketch for the "Mothers of America" stamp is shown here. In 1933 Mrs. H. H. McCluer, a past national president of the American War Mothers, conceived the idea of issuing a special stamp for use in conjunction with Mother's Day mail. She met with Roosevelt on January 25, 1934. Known to be a devoted son, the President granted her request three weeks later. The stamp was issued May 2, 1934.

In 1939, Roosevelt sketched this design on White House stationery for the "50 Years of Statehood" issue for Washington, South Dakota, North Dakota, and Montana. An example of the stamp, issued on November 2, 1939, appears above the president's sketch.

Rooselvelt's original drawing on White House stationery for the "50 Years of Statehood" issue for Washington, South Dakota, North Dakota, and Montana, with stamp as issued. *From the Smithsonian National Postal Museum collection.*

Roosevelt's original sketch for the "Mothers of America" stamp. *From the Smithsonian National Postal Museum collection.*

## 1959 Canada St. Lawrence Seaway

In 1959 Canada released a commemorative stamp for the St. Lawrence Seaway. As a bicolor stamp, the issue went through the presses twice. A small quantity of inverts were accidentally printed and distributed to Canadian post offices. Approximately sixty-two mint and used examples remain in the hands of collectors.

Canada's St. Lawrence Seaway stamp of 1959 with an inverted center. *From the Smithsonian National Postal Museum collection.*

United States 1979 rush lamp candleholder regular issue with an inverted candleholder. *From the Smithsonian National Postal Museum collection.*

Letter assigning American Sea Post Clerk Oscar Scott Woody to work on the maiden voyage of the ill-fated R.M.S. *Titanic*. *From the Smithsonian National Postal Museum collection.*

## The CIA Invert

The $1 Colonial Rush Lamp and Candle Holder stamp was first printed in 1979. In 1986 one hundred stamps with the inverted brown candleholder were sold to the public. Five of those stamps were presumed used on mail, with the invert error going undetected. Employees of the Central Intelligence Agency purchased the remaining 95. This stamp error soon became known as the "CIA invert."

## R.M.S. *Titanic* Objects

Two paper objects are illustrated from the sea post office aboard the R.M.S. *Titanic*. Both items were recovered from the body of American Sea Post clerk Oscar Scott Woody after the sinking of the vessel. The first item is the April 1, 1912 letter assigning him to work aboard the ship on its April 10 maiden voyage from Southampton, England, to New York City. The second is a facing slip used to route letters to Washington State and Alaska; it is stamped TITANIC, O S WOODY and postmarked TRANSATLANTIC POST OFFICE 7, AP 10 (19)12.

ABOVE RIGHT A facing slip used to route letters to Washington State and Alaska recovered from the body of Sea Post Clerk Woody after the sinking of the R.M.S. *Titanic*. BELOW: Pocket watch of John Starr March, who was a Sea Post Clerk on the fateful maiden voyage of the R.M.S. *Titanic*. It is corroded from having been in seawater. *Both images from the Smithsonian National Postal Museum collection.*

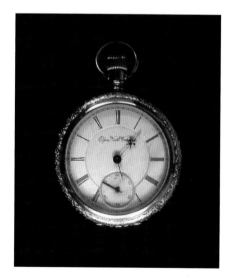

### CHAPTER TEN

# YOU ARE A STAMP COLLECTOR!

## What's Next?

You have begun noticing attractive stamps on your mail. You have purchased new stamps from the post office and set them aside because you "liked them." Maybe you have even gone online and purchased some stamps from an internet auction, and now joined to those stamps you have saved from your mail and the post office are others you have collected from various sources. Your small but growing collection gives you enjoyment, but you want more. Where do you go from here?

A beginning collector often receives well-meaning advice to "specialize" in some aspect of the stamp hobby. The specialization can be in a specific country, topic, time period, or branch of the stamp hobby. The most specialized of specialist collectors might only collect a single stamp issue.

In some ways, specializing makes sense. Completing a specialized collection is certainly more attainable with its narrow goals. Unfortunately, specialization also has some downsides. By selecting only one or two specialties, a collector limits his exposure to the richness, depth, and diversity that a worldwide stamp collector experiences.

Many, if not most, collectors begin as "general" or worldwide collectors. In this formative stage, any stamp from anywhere is of interest and gleefully added to the collection. Collecting

OPPOSITE: Mailboxes.

"everything" also has downsides. Just acquiring the stamp albums needed to house such a collection can easily exceed the limitations of both finances and shelf space and the odds are very small that a worldwide collector who sets completion as a goal will ever find success.

## Deciding What to Collect

Deciding whether to specialize in one aspect of the stamp hobby or be a general worldwide collector is not a decision a beginning or even intermediate collector needs to make. Collect what you like. Your interests should steer how you spend your time and money. Never allow others to dictate your collecting habits. Keep your mind open to new ideas in stamp collecting.

Collecting "everything you like" makes your stamp collection a unique reflection of you. Everything in it will be a joy for you to own, and your collection is always complete until you find the next stamp you like. Eventually what you collect may lead you toward one or more specialties. For example, in time you may find you delight in collecting stamps from Brazil. That would be a sure sign you are ready to specialize in that one country. Or, your longtime love for comic books could manifest itself in collecting stamps that portray cartoons, caricatures, and comics.

Even then, keeping a general worldwide collection going is not a bad idea. A worldwide collector can always find new stamps to add to the collection. It is surprising how many interesting stamps can be acquired on a tight budget. Collecting the world prods collectors to explore the hobby's byways as well as its highways. It gives participants a broad general knowledge of many subjects rather than specialized knowledge of only a few. A worldwide collection allows you to converse with others about a diverse range of collecting areas.

## How to Research a Stamp

Collecting stamps for the beauty of their design is satisfying, but every stamp has a story. Learning the story behind the stamp is even more fulfilling. Suddenly those little scraps of paper in your stamp albums come to life. They represent real people, moments in history, world events, and popular culture. An album full of stamps is a veritable treasure trove of high drama and crowning achievements waiting to be discovered by those curious enough to make the effort.

How do you find those stories? Where do you look?

The first place to look is a stamp catalog. In addition to the pertinent philatelic information about the stamp (type of printing, watermark, gauge of perforations, colors, and so on) there will usually be a brief description about what is illustrated on the stamp. Once armed with that data, it is easier to proceed with further investigation.

Illustrated here is an example using a very common 20 pfennig stamp from Bavaria, litho printed in deep blue on blue paper. It was issued in 1911. It bears a portrait of a bearded gentleman. Who is this man? The catalog identifies him as PRINCE REGENT LUITPOLD. The title "Prince Regent" is usually bestowed on an individual who rules a country instead of the monarch because the monarch is incapacitated in some way.

This stamp's story unfolded by consulting an encyclopedia for the listing for LUITPOLD. Prince

A 1911 stamp from Bavaria has a portrait of Prince Regent Luitpold.

Regent Luitpold was forced into the Bavarian regency against his will when his nephew King Louis II was found unfit to rule. A few days after Luitpold was named regent, King Louis II died. The succession would have gone to Luitpold's younger nephew Otto, but Otto was insane and unfit to reign.

Luitpold retained his title and reigned as Prince Regent of Bavaria for the next twenty-six years until his death, a period considered by historians to be the golden age of Bavaria. This common stamp reveals a story that sounds like a royal soap opera about the reluctant Luitpold and his unfit family.

That was an easy story to research that required only a stamp catalog and encyclopedia. Other stamps and covers have fascinating stories, but those stories may not be so easy to sleuth. The objective in researching any item in your collection is to answer the same questions asked by good journalists: who, what, where, when, why, and how.

Philatelic help is available through stamp collecting organizations, museums, and libraries. Many of these excellent groups have journals that might have answers to your questions. Stamp col-

lectors generously share their research with one another and often collaborate to produce the best possible results.

The internet is a great tool that will make research faster and easier, but personally visiting libraries, archives, and museums for primary documents is still the most thorough and satisfying method of historical research. Do not overlook the telephone and ordinary mail as research tools. Many hours of unproductive searching can be saved by making a telephone call or writing a letter to those most likely to have the information you seek.

### Smithsonian National Postal Museum

The Smithsonian National Postal Museum has much to offer stamp collectors and researchers. In recent years the philatelic galleries have exhibited a rotating array of exhibits, such as gems from Her Majesty Queen Elizabeth's collection that illustrated the development of the first postage stamp. Other exhibits document how the mail helped the United States grow and prosper and how mail delivery methods adapted throughout the years. Many of the exhibits are interactive, delighting children and adults alike.

The National Postal Museum Library is one of twenty specialized libraries in the Smithsonian Institution Libraries system. It is not a lending library, but researchers may make an appointment to use the more than 40,000 books, specialized catalogs, journals, auction catalogs, and archival materials. The National Postal Museum website (www.postalmuseum.si.edu) has wonderful content for serious researchers as well as those who are merely curious. There is more information there about the materials that are available to researchers and how to use them.

## Joining a Stamp Club

The common perception of a stamp collector is one who works in isolation, but the hobby is better enjoyed in the company of others. A local stamp club is a great place to meet other collectors, share knowledge and experience, learn about the hobby, and acquire new stamps. It can be intimidating to walk into a meeting where nearly everyone already knows everyone else, but everyone there was a stranger once, too.

Find a stamp club in your area by contacting the American Philatelic Society (see "Sources," this chapter), searching on the internet, or asking the local chamber of commerce or post office.

Stamp club meetings usually start with a short business meeting followed by a program. The program may be a slide show, a "how to" demonstration, a talk by one of the members, an auction, or a swap session. These main programs are often supplemented with trading between members, quizzes, door prize

A stamp show is a great place to make new friends, find new material for a stamp collection, and learn new things. Photo from the Washington 2006 World Philatelic Exhibition.

drawings, and the opportunity to purchase stamps from sales books. No matter what the program may be, it is an opportunity for you to increase your knowledge and make new friends.

Some clubs may have additional benefits. Many stamp clubs have newsletters that keep the membership informed of future meetings, shows, and other news of interest. Other clubs have established libraries of stamp catalogs and other references.

## Specialty Societies

Stamp collecting is like the trunk of a great tree off which many branches grow and prosper. Some stamp collectors concentrate on a particular country or topic. Others may devote their attention to a single stamp or the entire world. Nearly every special interest within the hobby has its own specialist society. Joining one or more of them will bring you in contact with others who share your exact interests.

Specialty societies publish journals or newsletters that highlight research and provide answers to questions. Many specialty societies conduct auctions for members to buy and sell material. The largest of the specialty societies have annual conventions, usually at a stamp show, where members give lectures and seminars. There are also social gatherings.

Finding a society that matches your interest is not difficult. (See "Sources" in this chapter.)

## Attending Stamp Shows

A stamp show is a microcosm of everything the stamp hobby offers: friendship, a learning experience, and the thrill of the hunt. Larger cities may have at least one stamp show each year. Shows come in many sizes and not all "stamp shows" have the same purpose.

Stamp bourses are commercial events where stamp dealers gather to sell stamps, covers, supplies, books, catalogs, and other items related to the stamp hobby. These may be large events with dozens of vendors or small with only four or five dealers offering their wares.

Stamp shows are nearly always sponsored by a stamp club or stamp federation. Stamp shows usually have exhibits in frames for visitors to enjoy, seminars or lectures on various topics, and stamp dealers from whom purchases may be made. Some of the largest stamp shows can be multi-day events that attract visitors from all over the world and have hundreds of stamp dealers.

The largest shows can be intimidating for new collectors or those who have never before been to a stamp show, but those who venture to a show are rewarded. Attending stamp shows is one of the most enjoyable aspects of the stamp hobby. A stamp show is a concentrated shopping mall where every store is catering to you by offering stamps, covers, and supplies that will enhance your collection. With so much to see and do it is best to plan your stamp show visit. Most shows, regardless of size, will have a program at the entrance. All of the dealers are listed, usually with an indication of the type of material they have for sale. Note those dealers who seem most likely to have what you seek. Do not forget to bring your want list.

It is perfectly acceptable to haggle a little over prices when you have found something you wish to purchase. It is never acceptable to insult the seller. A good approach is to ask simply, "What is your best price?" or "Will you come down on this price?" If the dealer's best price is still too high, the most effective response is "no, thanks." Insulting the dealer will not make him or her any more likely to lower the price. Do not feel obligated to purchase something you really do not want if you spend a lot of time looking through a dealer's stock and come up emptyhanded. Hand the material back to the dealer and thank him for allowing you to look.

Review the show program to see if there are any meetings or seminars that you want to attend. Often there will be slide programs or other talks that can be a tremendous opportunity to learn and meet other collectors.

If exhibits are part of the show, save some time to have a look at those. These exhibits have been assembled by collectors like you who want to share their treasures and research with other collectors. You would not go to a museum without looking at the displays. Do not go to a stamp show without looking at the stamps being shown.

Watch your budget. It is very easy to lose track of how much money you are spending. Keep a little notebook with you to write down the purchases you make. Keep a running total and when you hit the limit of your hobby spending, stop shopping and go to seminars or look at exhibits instead. There are plenty of free entertainments at the show. Try them all to multiply your enjoyment.

### Have Fun!

Never forget that stamp collecting is a fun hobby. You can collect stamps because they are beautiful, historically important, illustrate something that appeals to you, are a connection to the past, or any other reason that strikes your fancy.

Welcome to the world's greatest hobby!

## Sources
## Where to find more information

### Chapter One
**Selected reading:**
*The Queen's Stamps* by Nicholas Courtney. Published 2004 by Methuen.
*The Reform of the Post Office in the Victorian Era, 1837 to 1864.* Edited by Gavin Fryer and Clive Ackerman. Published 2000 by the Royal Philatelic Society, London.
*The Stamp Atlas* by Raife Wellsted, Stuart Rossiter, and John Flower. Published 1986 by Macdonald & Co.

**Selected websites:**
Smithsonian National Postal Museum:
www.postalmuseum.si.edu
British Library Philatelic Collection:
www.bl.uk/collections/stamps.html
History of the United States Postal Service:
www.usps.com/history/history/

### Chapter Two
**Selected reading:**
*Fundamentals of Philately* by L. N. Williams. Published 1990 by the American Philatelic Society.

### Chapter Four
**Selected vendors for supplies:**
American Philatelic Society
(reference books, stamp identifier, watermark fluid, *American Philatelist* magazine, magnifiers, many other services for members)
100 Match Factory Place
Bellefonte, PA 16823
www.stamps.org

Amos Hobby Publishing
(stock books, hinges, mounts, stamp tongs, perforation gauges, watermark fluid, stamp identifier, ultraviolet lamps, color guides, stamp albums, drying books, *Linn's Stamp News* weekly newspaper, *Scott Stamp Monthly* magazine, *Scott Standard Stamp Catalogues*)

P.O. Box 828
911 Vandemark Road
Sidney, OH 45365-0828
www.amosadvantage.com/scottonline/

Stanley Gibbons
(*Stanley Gibbons Stamp Catalogues, Gibbons Stamp Monthly* magazine, stamps, stamp auctions, albums, stock books, hinges and mounts, color guides, reference books)
399 Strand
London, WC2 0LX England
www.stanleygibbons.com

Subway Stamp Shop
(full range of stock books, stamp albums, reference works, stamp hinges and mounts, tongs, perforation gauges, watermarking supplies, ultraviolet lamps, color guides, drying books, glassine and polyester envelopes and bags, stock cards, and more)
2121 Beale Avenue
Altoona, PA 16601
www.subwaystampshop.com

### Chapter Five
**For help in finding stamp dealers:**
American Philatelic Society
100 Match Factory Place
Bellefonte, PA 16823
www.stamps.org/directories/dir_DealerMembers.htm

American Stamp Dealers Association
3 School Street
Suite 205
Glen Cove, NY 11542-2548
www.asdaonline.org

National Stamp Dealers Association
2916 N.W. Bucklin Hill Road #136
Silverdale, WA 98383-8514
www.nsdainc.org

Postal administrations:
United States Postal Service

Stamp Fulfillment Services
P.O. Box 219424
Kansas City, MO 64121-0924
www.usps.com

**Listings of worldwide postal administrations
are available on these websites:**
American Stamp Dealers Association
    www.asdaonline.com/index.php?id=21
Ask Phil
    www.askphil.org/b38a.htm
Linn's Stamp News
    http://www.linns.com/reference/postadmin/
    admins.asp

**Selected internet-based stamp auction websites:**
eBay
    www.ebay.com
Stamp Wants
    www.stampwants.com

Chapter Seven
**Selected reading:**
*How to Detect Damaged, Altered, and Repaired
    Stamps* by Paul W. Schmid. Published 1979
    by Palm Press.
*Out-Foxing the Fakers* by Jean-Francois Brun.
    English translation published in 1993 by the
    American Philatelic Society.
*Care and Preservation of Philatelic Materials* by T.
    J. Collings and R. F. Schooley-West. Published
    1990 by the British Library and the American
    Philatelic Society.
*Saving Stuff* by Don Williams and Louisa Jaggar.
    Published 2005 by Fireside Books.

**Selected websites:**
American Philatelic Society
Care and Preservation of Philatelic Materials
Committee Home Page
    www.stamps.org/CARE/Pcpm.htm

Smithsonian National Postal Museum
Preservation Primer for Collectors
    www.postalmuseum.si.edu/stamp/
    5d_preserving1.html

**Selected sources of preservation and archival
materials:**
Atlantic Protective Pouches
(protective polyester sleeves)
P.O. Box 1191
Toms River, NJ 08754
www.atlanticprotectivepouches.com

Gaylord Bros.
P.O. Box 4901
Syracuse, NY 13221-4901
www.gaylord.com

Metal Edge, Inc.
6340 Bandini Boulevaard
Commerce, CA 90040
www.metaledgeinc.com

University Products
517 Main Street
P.O. Box 101
Holyoke, MA 01040-0101
www.universityproducts.com

Chapter Eight
**Selected expertizing services:**
American Philatelic Expertizing Service (APEX)
100 Match Factory Place
Bellefonte, PA 16823
www.stamps.org/Services/ser_aboutexpertizing.htm

Association Internationale des Experts en Philatelie
Herzog-Friedrich-Straße 19
A-6020 Innsbruck
Austria
www.aiep-experts.net

Philatelic Foundation
70 West 40th Street, 15th Floor
New York, NY 10018
www.philatelicfoundation.org

Professional Stamp Experts (PSE)
P.O. Box 6170
Newport Beach, CA 92658
www.psestamp.com

Royal Philatelic Society London (RPSL)
41 Devonshire Place
London W1G 6JY England
www.rpsl.org.uk

Chapter Ten
**Selected research resources:**
American Philatelic Research Library
100 Match Factory Place
Bellefonte, PA 16823
www.stamplibrary.org

British Library Philatelic Collection
96 Euston Road
London NW1 2DB England
www.bl.uk/collections/stamps.html

Collectors Club (New York)
22 East 35th St.
New York, NY 10016-3806
www.collectorsclub.org

Rocky Mountain Philatelic Library
2038 South Pontiac Way
Denver, CO 80224
www.rockymountainphilateliclibrary.com

Smithsonian National Postal Museum Library
2 Massachusetts Avenue, N.E.
Washington, DC 20560-0570
www.sil.si.edu/libraries/npm

Spellman Museum of Stamps & Postal History
235 Wellesley Street
at Regis College
Weston, MA 02493
www.spellman.org

Wineburgh Philatelic Research Library
P.O. Box 830643
Richardson, TX 75093-0643
www.utdallas.edu/library/collections/speccoll/wprl
/wprl.htm

Western Philatelic Library
P.O. Box 2219
Sunnyvale, CA 94087-0219
www.pbbooks.com/wpl.htm

**Information on local stamp clubs, specialty societies and stamp shows:**
American Philatelic Society
100 Match Factory Place
Bellefonte, PA 16823
www.stamps.org

**General information sources on the Internet:**
Smithsonian National Postal Museum
    www.postalmuseum.si.edu
American Philatelic Society
    www.stamps.org
Ask Phil
    www.askphil.org
United States Postal Service
    www.usps.com

**Recommended reading:**
*Linn's World Stamp Almanac.* Published 2000 by
    *Linn's Stamp News*
*Encyclopedia of United States Stamps and Stamp
    Collecting*, Rodney A. Juell and Steven J.
    Rod, editors. Published 2006 by Kirk House
    Publishers.

# GLOSSARY OF TERMS
## USED IN THIS BOOK

**Advertising cover** An envelope illustrated to sell a product or service.

**Airmail stamps** Stamps that pay fees for airmail service for letters and parcels.

**Approvals** Method of purchasing stamps. Stamps are sent by a dealer to a potential customer who selects stamps to keep and returns the remaining stamps with a payment for those purchased.

**Auxiliary markings** Any instructional marking that appears on a piece of mail. Auxiliary markings include "return to sender," "deficient address," "moved, left no forwarding address," and many others.

**Backstamps** Postal markings that appear on the back of an envelope. Backstamps are usually indicative of transit postal stations or the receiving post office.

**Bank mixture** Assortments of stamps that have been gleaned from the correspondence of banks and other commercial institutions that received lots of registered or certified mail bearing high-denomination stamps. Stamps will be on-paper.

**Banner** Any boxed area within a stamp design that contains text such as a country name, the identification of the main design element, or the type of service use of the stamp provides (such as airmail or special delivery).

**Bogus** A stamp, postmark, or cover that is a complete fabrication, perhaps designed to fool a stamp collector, but based on no known genuine example.

**Bourse** A venue for stamp dealers to assemble and sell their stamps, stamped envelopes, and supplies.

**Box Lots** An assortment of stamps, and sometimes stamped envelopes, contained in a box. Collectors should review a box lot in person, or carefully read the description to learn in better detail what the box contains.

**Bullseye** 1. Nickname for Brazil's first postage stamps issued August 4, 1843. The stamps had a large numeral within an oval that bore a resemblance to a "bull's eye."

2. Term used by stamp collectors to describe a postmark that is perfectly centered on a postage stamp. Stamp collectors also call this phenomenon a "socked on the nose" cancel, or use the acronym "SOTN."

**Cachets** An illustration applied to an envelope. Cachets may be printed, hand-drawn, hand-painted, computer generated, or applied in mixed media.

**Cachetmaker** A person who designs or prints illustrations on envelopes.

**Cancel** The part of a postmark that strikes the stamp, defacing it and invalidating it for further postal use.

**Canceled-to-order** Stamps canceled by postal authorities without doing postal service. Also sometimes called "favor canceled." Canceled-to-order stamps are frequently sold by postal administrations to stamp dealers at a discount from face value.

**Censored mail** Mail that has been examined by a person authorized to inspect it to determine if the contents disclose sensitive information or contraband.

**Censorship markings** Handstamps, labels, seals, or other indication applied to an envelope, postcard or parcel to show that the mail piece has been inspected by a censor.

**Certified mail** An added-fee service similar to registration in that it is a secure method to send letters or parcels with a receipt for proof of mailing and delivery, but carries no compensation for loss or damage.

**Cinderellas** Stamplike items that have no postal validity.

**Coil stamps** Stamps that have been made into coiled rolls, primarily to accommodate stamp vending machines and stamp affixing machines.

**Collection** A grouping of stamps organized and formed into some sort of cohesive unit by a collector.

**Color guide, color key** Color chips, cards, or folders showing blocks of color that have been identified with color names. A stamp is placed next to the color chip and compared until a matching color is found.

**Comb perforations** Perforations made to at least three sides of a stamp at once. Stamps with comb perforations usually have corner perforations that align with no overlap.

**Commemorative stamps** Stamps created to honor a person, place, thing, historic anniversary, or event. These stamps are usually on sale for a limited period of time.

**Convertible stamp booklets** Double-sided sheet of self-adhesive stamps. The sheet can be folded into thirds without damaging any of the stamps, making a tight package that fits easily into a wallet.

**Counterfeit** An imitation of a genuine stamp, overprint, surcharge, postal marking, or cancellation. Used interchangeably with "forgery."

**Cover** Outer covering of a letter or other mail piece. This usually refers to an envelope, but may also be used for parcel boxes or other forms of wrapper.

**Crash cover** An envelope that survived an airline, airship, rail, or motor vehicle crash. Salvageable crash mail is usually marked prior to forwarding it to the recipient.

**Dead Country** A country or former stamp-issuing entity that no longer issues its own postage stamps.

**Denomination** The value printed on the stamp.

**Discontinued post office, DPO** A post office that has been closed by the postal administration.

**Double Geneva** Nickname for stamps first issued by the Swiss canton of Geneva on September 30, 1843. The stamps were created on sheetlets of two stamps. A postal patron could mail a local letter using one of the stamps to pay the postal fees, or mail a letter outside the local area but still within the canton by using both of the stamps on the sheetlet to pay the proper fee.

**Embossing** A method of raising a part of a stamp design above the surface of the paper.

**Entire** A completely intact stampless letter, folded letter sheet, or item of postal stationery.

**Error** A major mistake in production or design of a stamp. The famous 24 cent inverted center Jenny biplane airmail stamp is an example of an error.

**Essay** A proposed or prototype stamp design created by the artist or designer for review by postal authorities. An essay may be rejected or approved in a modified form for a stamp design.

**Etiquette** A label applied to a piece of mail that indicates a type of service, such as airmail, registered mail, or special delivery.

**Event covers** Illustrated envelopes designed to mark a particular event. The envelope will be stamped and there will usually be a complementary cancel.

**Express Mail stamps** Stamps issued to indicate payment has been received for Express Mail service available in the United States and some other countries. The service guarantees next day delivery for most addresses.

**Extension** A term used by auctions to describe a hold on transfer of ownership, pending expertization.

**Facsimile** An imitation of a stamp that has been made to look like a genuine but was not printed from the original plates, when there has been no intent by its creator to defraud.

**Fake** A stamp, cover, or other philatelic item that has been altered or tampered with in some way to trick collectors into believing it is more valuable or desirable.

**Fancy cancels** A generic term used to describe any cancel that is elaborate or pictorial.

**First day cover, FDC** An envelope bearing a newly issued stamp postmarked on the first day it was placed on sale. The envelopes often have an illustration that relates to the stamp.

**First Day of Issue** The first day a new stamp is placed on sale.

**First issues** The first stamp or stamps released by a country. Great Britain's Penny Black was that country's first issue. The United States's first issues were the 5 cent Franklin and 10 cent Washington stamps of 1847.

**Forever stamps** Nondenominated stamps sold by the post office at the prevailing rate that will satisfy the payment for sending the specified class of mail into the future regardless of postal rate increases.

**Forgery** An imitation of a genuine stamp, overprint, surcharge, postal marking, or cancellation. Used interchangeably with "counterfeit."

**Freak** A minor, non-reoccurring mistake or variety. These can have spectacular appearance, such as a shifted color or a stamp that has been misperforated.

**Frame** The outer area of a stamp that usually contains the secondary elements of the stamp design such as country name and denomination.

**Frank** The handwritten notation, handstamp, adhesive stamp, meter stamp, or imprint on a cover that advises postage has been paid.

**Franking privilege, free frank** A postal inscription, usually the signature of the sender or the written word FREE that indicates the sender has the authority to send the letter without incurring postal fees.

**Grade** Refers to how well the stamp is centered within the margins.

**Gravure, photogravure** A type of recess printing that uses a photographic process to create a printing plate. The process creates small dots of color that can be seen with magnification. This method is often used to create multicolored stamps.

**Handstamp** A postal marking that was applied by hand rather than by machine.

**Harrow perforations** Type of perforation that perforates a whole sheet of stamps at once.

**Hinges** Small rectangular pieces of gummed glassine paper used to secure stamps in stamp albums.

**Intaglio, line engraving, engraving, recess printing** Method of printing that uses printing plates made from a metal die into which the design had been etched or engraved. The engraving of the die could have been done by hand or by a lathe machine. Machine engraving is called "engine-turned." Intaglio printing is crisp, finely detailed, and the ink is raised slightly above the paper.

**Joint issues** Stamps issued by two or more postal administrations with identical or similar designs. The stamps commemorate a person or event of common interest, and are usually released on the same day or within a few days of one another.

**Key-plate stamps/Keytype stamps** Postage stamps used in small colonies or countries that bear a generic design and an area where the country name and denomination were added using another printing plate. The basic design could be printed in quantity and used indiscriminately for any of the participating colonies.

**Kiloware** A stamp mixture sold by weight. A kilogram is about 2.33 pounds. Some U.S. dealers sell kiloware by the pound or fraction thereof.

**Letterpress, typographic printing** A method of printing from a plate that has a raised design. The raised areas are inked and pressed into the paper. This results in solid printed areas that are slightly impressed into the paper.

**Line perforations** Perforations made in straight lines, one or more line at a time. Line perforations often overlap at the corners.

**Lithography, surface printing, chromolithography, photolithography** Printing method that uses chemically treated plates that accept or reject ink areas to be printed. Stamps that have been printed by lithography have very flat printing and solid areas of color.

**Local stamps** Stamps for use in a specific region or a limited postal system. These may be issued officially by postal authorities or unofficially by private carriers or corporations.

**Microprinting** Letters, symbols, or words printed in very small type that are incorporated into a stamp design as a security feature. The small type will not reproduce well or at all by using xerography or other photocopying methods.

**Military newspaper stamps** Stamps used to indicate payment has been made to send a newspaper to someone serving in the armed forces. These were generally sent at a much reduced concessionary rate for service personnel.

**Military stamps** Stamps that are used by active service personnel under a variety of circumstances, usually as part of a fighting force in war time or as part of an occupation force.

**Mint** Refers to stamps that have never been used and are in the same condition as when they were purchased at the post office, with full original gum and no trace of a stamp hinge.

**Mission mixture** Stamps collected by a charitable organization or other sources and sold in bulk to dealers. These mixtures are usually heavily duplicated and contain mostly small-sized regular issue stamps on-paper.

**Mixture** Generally, an assortment of stamps that may be worldwide, single country, regional, or thematic. A mixture will usually contain regular issue and commemorative stamps, often in duplication, and unless otherwise stated stamps will be both on- and off-paper and in mixed condition.

**Mounts** Double strips of polyester film or other inert plastic material that are heat-sealed on one or more sides, used to secure stamps in stamp albums.

**Newspaper stamps** Stamps used for reduced rate newspaper delivery made by a postal service.

**Newspaper tax stamps** Stamps that are used by a postal service to collect a compulsory tax on the delivery of foreign newspapers.

**Newspaper wrappers** Sheet of paper bearing an imprinted stamp that is wrapped around a newspaper and secured with a label or seal.

**Nondenominated stamps** Stamps that do not having a face value printed on the stamp.

**Occupation stamps** Stamps issued for use in nations or areas being occupied by military forces or government authorities of another nation.

**Off-paper mixture** An assortment of loose stamps that are no longer attached to pieces of envelopes. The stamps are ready to mount in an album or stock book.

**Official stamps** Stamps issued for use by authorized government departments and agencies.

**Omnibus stamps** A stamp or series of stamps issued by several postal entities to note a common theme. The stamps may have the same design, but it is not required.

**On-paper mixture** Contains clippings from envelopes and packages with the stamps still attached to paper from the envelopes.

**Original gum** Condition of a stamp's gum as distributed from the printer. Gum has no damage or hinge marks.

**Overprint** Any printing that is added on top of a stamp. An overprint can take many forms and serve many purposes.

**Pane** A subdivision of a sheet of stamps. Stamps are commonly printed on high-speed presses in very large sheets too big to handle at post offices. The sheets are subdivided, usually separated by blank areas called "gutters" and cut into more manageable sizes. When a postal customer buys a "sheet" of stamps at a post office, it is almost always a pane from a much larger sheet.

**Parcel post stamps** Stamps that indicate payment has been made by the sender for the required postage for packages sent. This special class of mail is usually a reduced rate.

**Patriotics** Envelopes illustrated with a patriotic theme.

**Penny Black** Nickname for the world's first adhesive postage stamp. It was printed in black by Perkins, Bacon, and Petch, British security printers. The stamp, bearing a portrait of Queen Victoria, was issued by Great Britain on May 6, 1840.

**Perforations** A stamp separation method in which a machine punches holes between stamp subjects in a sheet of stamps. The holes weaken the paper to make it easier to separate one stamp from another.

**Perfins** A stamp that has initials or other design perforated into the stamp's design area. This is a security method to prevent business or government employees from using the stamps for their private mail.

**Perforation gauge** A plastic, metal, or paper device used to measure the number of perforation "holes" along the sides of stamps.

**Personalized stamps** Stamps printed by postal authorities or authorized private firms that bear a customer-supplied picture or photograph. Personalized stamps are sold at higher than face value to cover expenses for printing.

**Philatelic forgeries** An imitation of a genuine stamp, overprint, surcharge, postal marking, or cancellation designed to deceive stamp collectors.

**Postage due/short paid letters** Stamplike adhesives that are used on letters and parcels with insufficient postage affixed. The recipient pays the amount of the shortage indicated by postage due stamps.

**Postal forgeries** An imitation of a genuine stamp designed to defraud the post office from fees required to pay for postal services.

**Postal fiscal stamps** Stamps that are used to indicate payment for a broad category of services including postage and fees or taxes for other kinds of governmental services such as deed or stock transfers, taxes on imported goods, and licensing and inspection fees.

**Postal history** The study of postal rates, routes, and postal markings.

**Postal rates** Prices charged by postal administrations for various services and delivery options.

**Postal tax stamps** Stamp that is affixed to a mail piece to indicate that payment of a compulsory government-mandated postal tax has been paid.

**Postmark** An official postal marking that usually provides the place, date, and often, the time a letter or parcel was mailed.

**Precancels** Stamps that have a printed or handstamped cancel applied before they are sold for use. Precancels are used for bulk mailings to eliminate the need for the post office to postmark the envelopes.

**Prepaid letter sheet** A sheet of paper issued by a postal administration or agency that has an imprint or indication that the postage fees have been paid by the purchaser. A letter is written on one side of the sheet. The letter sheet is then folded, sealed, and mailed.

**Provisional stamps** Stamps that fill a short-term need or requirement for new denomination, usually as a result of a postal rate change.

**Railway newspaper stamps** Stamps issued by government agencies to show payment of freight charges for newspapers carried by rail.

**Registered mail** An added-fee service for sending a letter or parcel securely. Registered mail receives a unique number that allows tracking. The sender receives a receipt with the number on it and the recipient must sign a receipt upon delivery. Compensation is made by the post office should a registered letter or parcel becomes lost in transit.

**Regular issues, definitive stamps** "Workhorse" stamps issued by postal administration for ordinary day-to-day letters and parcels. Regular issues are in use for extended periods of time.

**Remainder collection** A stamp collection that has had the better items removed.

**Reprints** Stamps that have been reprinted from the original plates and often in the original colors, usually with the authorization of postal authorities.

**Revenue stamps** Stamps that are used to indicate payment of a wide variety of taxes. Revenue stamps have no postal function.

**Roulette** A stamp separation method in which a machine makes tightly spaced cuts between stamp subjects in a sheet of stamps. The cuts can be straight lines or in a pattern; they weaken the paper so that the stamps may be torn apart without using scissors.

**Self-adhesive stamp** Stamp having gum that does not require moisture. These stamps generally have a peelable backing that must be removed before applying the stamp to an envelope or parcel. The stamp will stick instantly to any paper once the backing has been removed.

**Semi-postal stamps** Stamps that carry with them an additional fee over and above those collected for postal services that is given to a designated charity.

**Se-tenant stamps** Two or more stamps with different designs that are joined together. Stamp collectors prefer that se-tenant stamps remain intact.

**Sheet** The unit of stamps that comes off the printing press, usually containing several hundred stamps.

**Souvenir sheets, miniature sheets** A sheet that contains one or more postage stamps related to a specific theme, along with decorative elements printed in the margins outside the stamp area. The decorative elements have no postal validity.

**Special delivery stamps** Stamps used on an expedited service that delivers a letter or parcel immediately upon arrival at the destination post office. Such mail does not have to wait for the next regular delivery.

**Stamp album** A bound or loose-leaf book with pages used to house and display stamps and covers.

**Stamp booklets** Small panes of stamps bound, sometimes with interleaving, into a booklet with paper covers. This creates a convenient way to carry stamps in wallets or handbags.

**Stamp catalog** Reference work, either printed or digitally delivered, that contains pertinent information about stamps. The information may include pictures of the stamps, gauge of perforations, method of printing, date of issue, type of watermark, varieties known to exist, and pricing.

**Stamp identifier** A reference work that contains illustrations and text to help stamp collectors determine the country from which a stamp was issued. This is especially useful for stamps that are identified by symbols instead of country names or those that have alphabets that are difficult for English speakers to decipher.

**Stamp tongs** A tweezers-like metal device used to grasp stamps. The use of stamp tongs protects stamps from becoming soiled in handling.

**Stampless letter or stampless entire** Folded letter-sheets upon which a message or letter has been written. The sheets are folded in such a way to provide a space for the address of the recipient. The letter is sealed with a wax wafer or sealing wax. When posted, the portion of the entire bearing the address is marked with the place of mailing and the amount of postage to be collected from the recipient or paid by the sender. Other postal markings may be added.

**Stamp show** An exposition of stamp exhibits, stamp dealers, and frequently lectures and seminars. Stamp shows will frequently have seminars or activities for adult beginners and youth.

**Stock book** An unprinted album with pages that bear polyester or glassine strips that hold stamps in place. Stamps may be moved at will without using mounts and without causing damage to the gum.

**Surcharge** An overprint that changes the original face value of a stamp.

**Sweatbox** A sealed container that introduces a controlled amount of humidity to a stamp or envelope. This device can be used to flatten creases, remove stamps from envelopes, or remove hinges from stamps.

**Swiss Cantonals** Stamps issued by cantons (or "states") within Switzerland between 1843 and 1850, when stamps for the entire federation of Switzerland replaced cantonals.

**Tagging** Phosphorescent coating added to a stamp that, when detected by automatic mail sorting equipment, aids in "facing" the mail and applying the cancel in the proper place to strike the stamps.

**Telegraph stamps** Stamps used to prepay the fees for sending a telegram.

**Tete beche** Two or more stamps where at least one stamp has been printed upside-down in relation to the stamp next to it. Tete beche stamps must be collected in unseparated pairs because to separate them would eliminate the tete beche feature.

**Tie, tied** A cancel or postmark that strikes both the stamp and the envelope to which it is attached.

**Transit markings** Postmarks applied to an envelope by a post office along a route that receives the letter and forwards it to the delivery post office or the next office along the route. Transit markings may appear on the front or back of an envelope, parcel, or card.

**Ultraviolet lamp** Electric device fitted with a light bulb that emits ultraviolet light required to view phosphorescence and luminescence on stamps.

**Universal Postal Union, UPU** An international organization whose mission is to maintain efficient exchange of mail between member nations.

**Unsorted** A mixture that is sold just as it was received from the source. The high values, commemoratives, or other more desirable stamps have not been "cherry-picked" from the mixture, nor have the obviously damaged stamps been culled.

**Used** Refers to stamps that have been affixed to a letter and parcel and traveled through the mail system.

**Value tablet** Defined portion of the stamp that contains the denomination.

**Variety** A stamp that differs in some way from the normal stamp of the same issue.

**Vignette** Central portion of a stamp design that is the main design element.

**Want list** A collector-made inventory of stamps needed for his or her collection. A want list will usually contain country name, catalog number, and other requirements.

**War tax stamps** Stamp that is used on letters and parcels to show payment has been made of a compulsory postal tax to support an armed conflict.

**Watermark** Slight thinning of paper that is deliberately made as a pattern during its manufacture. A watermark serves as a security device against forgery.

**Watermark fluid and tray** The two items most commonly used to make hard-to-see watermarks visible. Watermark fluid is sold under several brand names. Commercially manufactured trays are also available, but any small, clean, shallow black glass or plastic tray will work.

# CREDITS

❧

My thanks to the extraordinary staff of the Smithsonian National Postal Museum for their help, support and encouragement:

The late W. Wilson Hulme II, Chief Curator of Philately; Cheryl Ganz, Ph.D., Curator of Philately; Daniel Piazza, Blount Research Chair; Nancy Pope, Historian; Allison Marsh, Assistant Curator; Linda Edquist, Conservator; Manda Kowalczyk, Preservation Technician; Helen Young, Conservator; Allison Gallaway, Public Affairs Officer; Elizabeth Schorr, Accessions Officer; Ted Wilson, Registrar; and Bill Lommel and Jim O'Donnell, Museum Specialists, for assistance with illustrations.

I am honored to include illustrations from the collection of Her Majesty Queen Elizabeth II. Sincerest thanks to Her Majesty and the Keeper of the Queen's Collection, Mr. Michael Sefi.

Thank you to the staff of Band-f for their attention to the million details of publishing a book: f-Stop Fitzgerald, Karen Jones, and Mie Kingsley.

Thanks to Yossi Malamud for help with illustrations and advice about stamps that have separate licensing issues, and to Ed Kawasaki and Andree Trommer-Schlitz for photographs from the Washington 2006 World Philatelic Exhibition.

Thank you to my sister-in-law Pat Cadena who reviewed this as a non-collector while it was a work in progress. She helped find text that might be unclear to beginners.


Band-f would like to thank Neil Segal at Colonial Stamp and Coin store, Kingston, NY; Postmasters Nora Collins, Judy Clark, Kathleen Styles, and Annie Mardiney at Rosendale, NY post office; and Weston Minissali of Preferably Tapioca LLC for digital scans.